Olive Oil

From Tree to Table

by Peggy Knickerbocker

Photographs by Laurie Smith

Foreword by Maggie Blyth Klein

CHRONICLE BOOKS

SAN FRANCISCO

Our special thanks to the late *Arlene Wanderman* of the International Council of Olive Oil, Foodcom, Inc.; Dun Gifford, Robin Insley, and Sara Baer-Sinnot of Oldways Preservation and Exchange Trust; and the California Olive Oil Council. Thanks to the Greek Food and Wine Institute, Foods from Spain, and the International Council of Olive Oil for providing information and travel for research.

Thanks to Paula Wolfert, Annie Lamott, Maggie Klein, Faith Willinger, Nancy Harmon Jenkins, Tony Knickerbocker, Shannon Kelly, Paul Bertolli, Joe Simone, Angelo Garro, Roberto Zecca, Francesca Zecca Applegarth, Walter Nicolau, Christopher Hirsheimer, Nancy Lesczcynski and Charles Ewell at Borro al Fumo, Robert Schneider, Reed Hearon, Gerald Hirigoyen, Mort Rosenblum, Mary Risley, Linda Golliber, Christina Salas-Porras, Sue Conley, Hoppin' John Taylor, M.F.K. Cowden, E.M. Ginger, Terry Gamble, Zarela Martinez, Patrick McFarlin, Ethel Bailey, Jody and Jonathan Schwartz, Catherine Brandel, Darrell Corti, Carolyn Zecca Ferris, Patty Dinner, Victoria Shoemaker, Bill LeBlond, Leslie Jonath, and Sharon Silva.

Peggy Knickerbocker would like to thank Laurie Smith for her remarkable eye and collaborative spirit.

Library of Congress Cataloging-in-Publication Data:
Knickerbocker, Peggy.
Olive oil: from tree to table/by Peggy Knickerbocker; photographs by Laurie Smith.
p. cm.
Includes bibliographical references and index.
ISBN 0-8118-1350-9 (pb)
1. Cookery (Olive oil) 2. Olive oil. I. Title.
TX819.O42K55 1997
641.6'463—dc21   96-48843 CIP
Printed in Hong Kong.

Designed by Yumiko Nakagawa
Illustrations by Diana Reiss-Koncar

Distributed in Canada by Raincoast Books
8680 Cambie Street
Vancouver, British Columbia V6P 6M9
10 9 8 7 6 5 4 3 2 1

Chronicle Books
85 Second Street
San Francisco, California 94105

Web Site: www.chronbooks.com

DEDICATION

To Bobby and Jamie

LAURIE SMITH

To the memory of my mother, Nancy, a good cook;
my father, Paine, a good writer; and to Tony and Marti

PEGGY KNICKERBOCKER

Contents

Foreword

It is impossible to think of the Mediterranean without the olive tree, rising gnarled from a parched, rocky, calcareous soil, its silvery green leaves shimmering against a gaudy azure sky. Giver of light and solace, nourishment and blessedness, the fruit of the olive has also brought a flavor unique to the cuisines of the birthplace of Western civilization.

It is miraculous that ancient peoples, who didn't have the technology we moderns consider ourselves fortunate to have, were able to devise methods by which to extract the oil that so enriched their lives. Nevertheless, as early as thirty-five hundred years ago, the seemingly unpromising and inedible little fruit was tapped for its oil. The use of olive oil seems to have been nearly synchronous with the beginnings of Western civilization itself. Because Eastern peoples managed to develop an equally civilized, complex, and highly evolved society without the discovery of olive oil, I will refrain from drawing what would otherwise be an obvious conclusion: that the achievements of Western man were brought about as a result of his having olive oil to light his nights, give solace and meaning to life, and brighten his table.

It is not known for a certainty where *Olea europaea*, the only species of the olive family of trees cultivated for its fruit, first sprang, or how it was developed. But it is generally thought to have been grown originally at about the same time in two places, namely, in Crete and in Syria, and to have derived from the wild species *Olea chrysophylla*. From Syria, the olive spread south and west

through northern Africa—with all of its peoples retaining the Semitic name *zait* for the fruit—and north and west to a much lesser extent. From Crete, the olive traveled north and west through southern Europe, the Greek word for olive, *elaiwa*, becoming *elia*, *maslina*, *olajbogyo*, *oliva*, and *olive* as it moved westward.

Evidence points to the olive being cultivated on Crete as early as 2500 B.C. A remarkable feature at the palace of Knossos was the Room of the Olive Press, with open pipes that fed into storage vats. Early on, the Minoans exported not only their olive oil, but also olive cuttings to the north coast of Africa and to Greece.

It was the Greeks who raised the olive and its oil to a place in their culture unrivaled by any other substance, plant, or food. Greek mythology describes a competition conducted by Zeus that would award patronage of Attica to the god or goddess who created the most useful gift. Poseidon gave the horse, powerful, swift, and beautiful; Athena produced the olive tree, with its light-giving, soothing (and delicious) oil, welcome shade, and valuable wood. Athena became the patron of Attica, and her gift, the City Olive, was

6

planted atop the Acropolis. It regenerated itself after invading Persians torched it, and its offshoots were planted throughout the region. Harming any of the new trees was made a capital offense. Throughout Greece, the olive branch and olive oil became symbolic of all that was good and noble in mankind, and of permanence and perseverance.

Olive oil became part of everyday activities, ceremonies, celebrations, and religious observances of the residents of the city-state. Before and after long journeys on foot, travelers applied olive oil to their feet. Professional masseurs in the public gymnasiums and baths were paid to rub customers with olive oil. Anointment became a sign of respect. People attending banquets wore olive wreaths, and were anointed with olive oil infused with spices and aromatics. The birth of a male child was announced at his parents' front door with an olive wreath. Olive branches became the emblems of supplicants and heralds, and therefore symbolic of nonviolence and harbingers of good things to come.

Athletes rubbed their bodies with oil before any exertion; after they cleansed themselves with lye and water, they rubbed themselves again with oil. The oil that was scraped from the bodies of the greatest athletes was thought to have certain powers and commanded a high price. Victors at the Olympic games were given oil in special *lecythi*.

Just as *Olea europaea* became central to the lives of the Greeks, so, too, was it embraced by the inhabitants of the land of Canaan. There, in addition to its oil becoming widely used for lamp fuel and in cooking, curatives, and salves, it became an essential ingredient in holy anointment. Exodus 30:22-33 reads: " . . . the Lord spake unto Moses, saying, take thou also unto thee

principal spices . . . and . . . olive oil. . . . And thou shalt make it . . . a holy anointing oil." To this day, Jewish synagogues and most Christian churches use the olive-based oil at many ceremonies.

The very word *Christ* means "anointed," and comes from *chrism*, which means "to anoint with oil" in Greek. The alabaster box of the Gospels is undoubtedly an alabastrum, or small olive oil flask from Greek and Roman cultures. And Noah's dove brought an emblem not only of peace, but also of regeneration with its olive twig (a sign, too, for Christians, that prefigured the resurrection).

The monarchs of Europe took over the practice of anointment with holy oil at their coronations. Through the centuries, the connotation of this ritual has changed to its current significance in England of bestowing strength and wisdom and a peaceful reign rather than absolute authority.

Being the rational, modern persons that we are today, we need no longer rub our dinner guests with oil or crown them with olive wreaths to show them our respect. All we need do is correct the Roman adage for a good life, "Wine within and oil without," to say, "Wine within . . . and oil within," and take care to supply our friends with a meal rich with the flavor and fragrance of fine olive oils. And Peggy Knickerbocker's splendid treatise and cookery book is just the compendium to enable the host to do exactly that.

Maggie Blyth Klein
Co-owner, Oliveto Restaurant
Author, The Feast of the Olive

Introduction

I have not *always* had twenty-four bottles of extra-virgin olive oil in a cool, dark spot in my kitchen. In fact, until a few years ago, I often bought only one bottle at a time. I had followed my parents' example, and that of the good cooks I had grown up with, buying, year in, year out, half gallons of the same kind of olive oil.

Saturdays were olive oil days around our house when I was growing up, which is to say that we used olive oil as an excuse to go to North Beach, the Italian part of San Francisco, since it was a livelier neighborhood than our own. There we'd buy a half gallon of Bertolli olive oil and come home to our flat on Pacific Avenue to funnel the oil into recycled red-wine bottles. Then we'd be ready for our weekend ritual.

My father was the olive oil maestro. Every other Saturday he would make mayonnaise by hand. It was a big production: he'd spread out the scant Saturday paper on our green wooden kitchen table and set the stage for his mayonnaise routine.

First he'd open the *New Yorker* to a lengthy story, the pages of which could be easily turned with one hand. The other hand would thus be free to beat the room-temperature eggs, dry mustard, lemon juice, salt, pepper, and olive oil in his old-fashioned hand device. It was a tall jar with an inverted lid that had a hole in it through which the plunger and the olive oil went. It took forever. He'd always complain of a sore arm. I'd offer to help, but he'd say that the rhythm would be interrupted if the procedure changed hands, that the mayonnaise might break. But he would let me pour, in a steady, thin thread, the golden oil, precisely measured in a special cup, through the tiny opening. My fascination with olive oil began during those mayonnaise mornings long ago.

When the mayonnaise was done, it was thick, lemony, flecked with black pepper, and richly yellow. Then we'd all have lunch together. The mayonnaise went so well on everything—cracked crab, a wobbly tomato aspic, chilled asparagus spears, and steamed artichokes. There would also be a big green salad dressed with a vinaigrette that my father had also made—again with Bertolli.

I often wonder what my father would think of my extravagant olive oil collection—some two dozen bottles standing in a cool corner of my kitchen, ready to be enlisted into action. He never changed brands. It was always Bertolli, in its pewter and copper can, consistent if not exquisite.

(I learned later that the intent of such big producers as Bertolli was to make a consistent oil, an oil that, year after year, could be counted upon to make mayonnaises and vinaigrettes taste the way cooks were used to having them taste. Never mind that the label would read "product of Italy"; the end result was inevitably a blend of oils that came not only from Italy, but from Spain, Greece, and maybe even Tunisia or Turkey. As long as an oil is packed in Italy, it is perfectly legal for the label to read "product of Italy.")

Once I had left the fold to open a couple of restaurants and a catering business, I went through cases of olive oil every year. Still young enough to be amused by the term *extra-virgin*, I was also a bit more of a culinary risk taker than my parents. When I opened Pier 23 Cafe in San Francisco, I arranged a display of fancy olive oil cans on the shelf that divided the kitchen from the customers. I was so fond of a ferocious tiger on one label that I assembled the patterns of the roaring mouth and the attacking paw in a line, like the legs of the Rockettes dancing across the stage at Rockefeller Center. But it wasn't until I started writing a few years back, when I began to travel and learn more about foods in other places, that I became aware of the nuances of fine olive oil. By no stretch of the imagination was our family's favorite brand the equivalent of Wonder bread, however. It was a perfectly decent olive oil, but I realized that there was also so much more out there.

And then it slowly became clear that there is an olive oil culture. Practically everywhere in the Mediterranean, the oil is regarded in almost religious terms. It's even called *olio santo* in Italy, and is reverentially used to "anoint" and "baptize" foods. In Morocco I saw millions of olive orchards, the trees lined up like soldiers about to march off toward the dry desert horizon. I went to Spain, Italy, and Greece—practically everywhere that great oils are pressed—and each step of the way I gathered recipes, new cooking techniques, and intriguing olive oil tales.

In recent years, olive oil has crept into the food pages of newspapers and magazines around the world. It began to replace butter, the previous staple of good cooks, and it appeared in little dishes on tables in fancy restaurants in the United States. Just about everything about olive oil was suddenly easy to swallow: its truly astonishing (if ever-changing) health claims, its great taste, and its appealing texture. But then there was a backlash—a puritanical overreaction to fat. The good, bad, low, and, finally, no-fat craze hit this country with an unambiguous assault. During that period, people started talking about being bad or sinful if they added an extra tablespoon of oil to a recipe. You might have thought, from the expression of horror on some dieters' faces, that it was malathion. I admit I succumbed to the pressure and set olive oil aside for a while, too. But when I ate my body weight in carbohydrates, and never lost a pound, it was time for olive oil again.

Strangely, I noticed that every time I traveled to the Mediterranean and ate a reasonable amount of sensational food, invariably cooked in olive oil, I came home a few pounds lighter. I began to take note of how traditional regional meals were made. They'd be simple, with fine fresh ingredients, but also be laced with olive oil, often olive oil I had not imagined in my sweetest dreams. Green, peppery, earthy oil from Tuscany, poured over a garlic-rubbed slab of grilled bread; ripe, yellow, grassy oil drizzled over a classic Greek salad; burnt orange Andalusian oil splashed in a pan to fry Iberian ham and partridge croquettes; a full, fruity, herbaceous Apulian oil, bringing to life a spring stew of favas, artichoke hearts, and crisp asparagus tips; or a stream of faintly fruity Lake Garda oil guided over a platter of grilled, delicate lake fish.

I'd leave the table satisfied with good food and inspired conversation. And I never needed to nibble between meals because I got what my stomach and soul craved: salt, sugar, oil, and protein in small measure, and good carbo-hydrates, vegetables, and fruits in profusion. My Mediterranean friends would ask about America's low-fat obsession, questioning why everyone couldn't simply eat smaller amounts of the best food and oil available, won-dering why they were so thin and Americans were so fat.

I started bringing home olive oils and recipes from Apulia and Tuscany, from Andalusia and Catalonia, and from Athens, Crete, and the Peloponnese. I collected ideas from my favorite cooks and chefs at home, in New York, in Los Angeles, and in Boston—people who understand and skillfully incor-porate olive oil into their repertoires. I wanted recipes that would flatter olive oil, that would be accommodating and inspirational to American chefs. When I began this book, Paula Wolfert, one of America's great cook-book writers, offered me an important piece of advice, "Only include recipes that you are absolutely in love with." And I have.

In assembling the recipes, I have sometimes suggested what kind of oil to use. Greek oil with Greek food would be the best way to go, of course, but if you only have a fine Tuscan oil, it will still taste good on a classic Greek salad. After all, the ingredients are Mediterranean. I encourage the tasting of and experimenting with as many oils as possible. Seeking out great olive oils when you travel is an excellent way to start. Ask questions, request tastes, and seek suggestions for cooking. Buy bottles of wonderful extra-vir-gin olive oil as you would wine (they'll last longer than one meal), incor-porate them into your recipes, fall in love with them.

Preceding the recipes, I have charted an olive oil voyage from the tree to the table—how and where olive trees grow, how the fruits are harvested, crushed, pressed, and bottled—with stops in the orchards and mills of Spain, Greece, and Italy.

Most people have a lot of questions about olive oil, and many of those are answered in this book. I suggest how to choose, buy, and store oil. I feel my state, California, is worthy of its own chapter, given its long history and renewed enthusiasm for olive oil. I have also taken a little extra space to dis-cuss frying and baking with olive oil, because until I started writing this book, I knew little about either technique.

But most of all I want cooks, after reading this book, to become passionate about olive oil the way I have. I want them to know what to look for in olive oil and then to urge purveyors to be honest and experimental with what they stock. Only then can American food lovers have an increased access to olive oil that one day might reflect its abundance and variety in the Mediterranean.

The Olive Tree

The olive tree has flourished for between three thousand and six thousand years in the Mediterranean. Its shallow roots grasp and bind the erosion-prone soil of many lands, just as its oil has formed and bound their cuisines. The Bible includes 140 references to olive oil, and it has symbolized longevity, fertility, maturity, and peace in various cultures. Olive oil has been a source of great wealth, an emblem of prosperity, the life blood of empires. It has been used as lamp fuel, a medicine, a hair and skin tonic, a balm to anoint sovereigns and priests, and even as a weapon (when it was boiled and poured over castle walls onto attacking hordes).

The World's Olive Oil Producers

Italy is the largest importer and exporter of olive oil in the European Community, yet Spain is the largest producer, accounting for 45 percent of the world's production. Italy follows with nearly 25 percent, and Greece with 20 percent. Most olive oil production in America occurs in California, yet the state is responsible for only .5 percent of the world's production. (Olive trees in Texas, Arizona, South America, and Australia account for far less.) Yearly, ten million metric tons of olives are harvested worldwide from nearly eight hundred million trees, nine million of which are used for olive oil; the remainder are cured as table olives.

14

Cultivation of the Olive

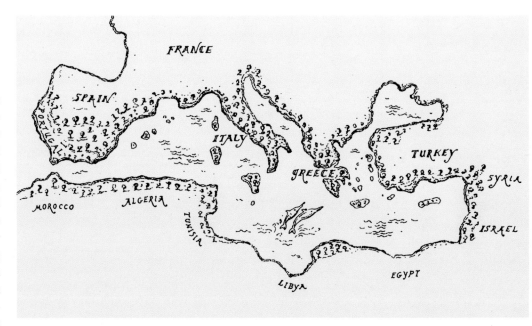

Throughout the Mediterranean, the olive tree is intertwined with the history of the region's people. Around 800 B.C., the Greeks and Phoenicians emigrated westward to Italy, France, Spain, and North Africa with shiploads of wheat, olives, and olive oil as currency for establishing trade with other Mediterranean civilizations. Today, we still see vast evidence of that diaspora. In Morocco and Tunisia, silver seas of olive trees stretch as far as the eye can see. In Spain, the trees march along the white, chalky plains of Andalusia, while in Italy, they encircle medieval villages in the Tuscan hills, and stand bold and gnarly among May poppies in the fields of Apulia. In Greece, endless groves creep past blue-trimmed white stucco houses down heathery coastal palisades to the sea. In Provence, the test of a properly pruned olive tree is if a swallow can fly through its branches without harming a wing.

The olive tree can withstand the starkest, bleakest conditions—long, hot summers, mild winters with little water, intense sun—adjusting its growing activity to a minimum in the face of either drought or excessive humidity. Poor soil can yield high-quality products, but so, too, can enriched soil. Olive trees are fairly low maintenance, requiring little irrigation or fertilization, and little pruning.

Wind also plays a major role in cultivation. It can be a curse in the spring, when the olive tree bursts forth with the tiny white flowers that will become its fruits, as strong winds can dislodge the buds, thereby greatly reducing the crop.

Resistance to cold is a varietal trait of some olive trees. This hardy stock can exist in near-freezing conditions (provided the trees don't remain in that state for more than a few days),

a circumstance that induces a vegetative rest much like an abbreviated version of the long winter's nap of a hibernating grizzly bear. Freezing temperatures can also result in serious consequences, however, as occurred in Provence, the olive oil capital of France, where the crop is still making a weak recovery from devastating frosts in 1956 and 1985. There, many former olive growers found it more profitable to replace at least one-third of the damaged olive trees with more rapid-growing fruit trees and vines. (Olive trees can take a long time to bear enough fruit to make harvesting worthwhile.) That is why there is not much French olive oil on the market today, and most of what is produced in Provence is heartily consumed on the spot.

The olive trees crippled by the monumental frost of 1985 in Tuscany have made a more robust comeback, and are again producing some of the world's finest extra-virgin oils.

Geographical Distribution of the Olive Tree

The olive tree proliferates, in diminishing order, in Spain, Italy, Greece, Turkey, Tunisia, Portugal, Syria, Morocco, Algeria, Lebanon, Albania, France, Argentina, former Yugoslavia, Libya, Jordan, the United States, Egypt, Israel, Cyprus, Afghanistan, Iran, Iraq, and Peru. Australia is producing olive oil, too. The olive tree grows most successfully in the northern and southern hemispheres between latitudes 30 and 45.

15

The Harvest

During the fall and winter months, preoccupation with the ancient tradition of olive harvesting reverberates in the Mediterranean world. The olive groves rustle in a big, silvery green ocean from Portugal and Morocco in the West to Syria and Turkey in the East. There are certain similarities and many differences in the rituals of the harvest from country to country, region to region. The exact time and particular method of harvest are only two of the factors that influence the ultimate virtue of an olive oil.

Olives are harvested at various times and in certain locales for specific results and for climatic considerations. In Chianti, most olives are picked by hand when they are green and rosy and barely ripe, because an early frost might ruin the crop. Oils pressed from the Tuscan harvest, a standard around which many people adjust their palates, are often green and assertive, typically with a peppery bite at the back of the throat. The taste and aroma of an exemplary Tuscan oil, made with a mixture of green and red-black olives, brings back memories of a youthful roll down a freshly mowed hill of grass. Ligurians harvest olives by hand as they fall into nets stretched under the trees when the olive is ripe and sweet—just like their oil. Olive trees grow slowly, taking from five to seven years to bear enough fruit to produce a feasible harvest, and even then each tree only produces three to four quarts of oil.

Since olives have a tendency to bruise if they drop to the ground, hand picking is the preferred method of harvesting. Bruising can cause oxidation and fermentation of the fruit, resulting in an oil with high acidity. This affects the taste and quality of the oil. Hand picking is labor intensive and expensive and is just one of the reasons for the high cost of olive oil.

In parts of Sicily, the tree branches are hit with a hazelnut stick or a pole, which causes the fruits to fall on tarps on the ground surrounding the trunk. In the Veneto and Tuscany, and other parts of the olive-producing world, it's not uncommon to see men using bright blue or orange plastic rakes—the kind children play with at the beach—to strip the branches of their olives. This is called combing the tree.

In Greece, where the oil is often fruity and complex, black plastic netting carpets the ground beneath the trees, providing a resting place for the fallen ripe olives. In parts of Andalusia, pickers strap wicker baskets around their necks to hold the hand-picked ripe black olives, which are tinged with a burnt almond flavor. In other parts of Spain, if the land is flat, automatic shakers clamp the tree trunk or big branches and vibrate the olives off. In Tunisia, the largest North African producer of olive oil, pickers attach goats' horns to their fingers, forming a clawlike contraption to hand-comb the olives off the branches. Much of Tunisia's olive crop is exported to France and bottled as a French product.

Today an increasing number of olives are harvested by machine—vibrating claws on tractors—but there are still many farmers who rely on methods that have been used for centuries, and most small-estate producers of fancy oils continue to harvest their olives by hand.

The Harvest in Chianti

During the olive harvest in Chianti, the landscape is devoid of color, except for the faint rusty tint of the trees standing out on the distant hills in the cold mist of early winter. The air is filled with an earthy, damp, fruity aroma. In northern Italy in the Veneto and in the hill towns of Chianti, I was reminded of one of Degas's ballet oils, painted from the perspective of the orchestra pit, where the viewer sees only the dancers' legs. Amid the olive trees I saw only legs on ladders— upper torso buried, hard at work in the arms of the tree. And no matter where I went, the women were always on the ground doing the backbreaking work of picking up the fallen fruits.

Liquid Gold

One year, about a month after the Greek tourist season ended in late fall, I toured the island of Crete and the Mani Peninsula in the Peloponnese, the country's two largest olive-producing regions, to check out the Greek olive harvest and to taste the food cooked with the new oil. The roads were teeming with trucks bulging with cartoonlike loads of olives on their way to cooperative mills. The chilly air was heavy with the scent of burning olive wood, a reminder of the pruning process that coincides with the harvest. The light was warm and rosy, and the sea sparkled and was mild enough for an early morning dip. Room-for-rent signs were still hung on tiny farmhouses, in hopes of eking out a few more tourist dollars. Black plastic netting covered the ground around the olive trees, awaiting the falling fruits, and stretched up over ancient stone walls like a Christo wrap.

In Greece, olive oil is almost as sacred as bread. It's sometimes given up during the high Lenten days, and urban government workers are allowed paid vacation time to return to their villages to help with family olive harvesting. The national average consumption is six to eight gallons per person per year. Yet despite the native demand, 80 percent of the Greek olive oil is bought by Spain and Italy.

In ports along the coast of the Peloponnese, I heard tales of gleaming stainless-steel trucks that dispensed olive oil into seafaring oil tankers bound for Italy and Spain. The sale of the oil resulted from fast and furious deals made by Italian and Spanish oil brokers with huge suitcases of ready cash. One of the reasons Americans don't know much about the splendors of Greek olive oil, or oils from Turkey and Tunisia, is that it's easy and tempting for the poor farmers to sell their oils to Italian bottlers for quick money. These oils are then, of course, sold as a product of Italy.

During my travels I met an Austrian, Fritz Blauel, who came to Greece almost twenty years ago, tasted the local oil of Kalamata, and decided to stay and make his own. He formed an organic co-op that required local olive farmers to refrain from using fertilizers and sprays. Since most of these farms were located in a tight little community, it was an all-or-nothing proposition: just one holdout could create chemical runoff that would contaminate the soil of organic neighbors. Blauel reminded reluctant farmers that for thousands of years their ancestors had taken the organic route.

On the morning we met, Blauel told me that one of the last people to join the organic concern was going to press her oil that day. She had diligently forgone any nonorganic activity for three years. He invited me to the ancient press to view the process and to taste her oil. She would save some for herself and the rest would be bottled under the Greek Gold label, olive oil usually available in whole-foods stores around the United States.

We arrived at the press on a chilly, gray afternoon. The olive farmer, Vangelia Hrisomalis, was dressed, like so many women of a certain age in Greece who have lost their husbands to war or old age, in black mourning garb. Vangelia dispatched orders to her sons and grandsons as they unloaded one of the bulging trucks filled with crate after crate of Koroneiki olives. (The familiar Greek Kalamata olives are table olives, not commonly used for oil.)

The olives were washed, deleafed, and then crushed by gargantuan stones that have been used for hundreds of years. The paste was further mixed to agglomerate the oil globules and obtain a separation of its different components. It was then spread onto hemp disks, every five or six of which were separated with supportive round steel plates. The resulting stack (like a pile of long-playing records on a phonograph spindle) was placed under a hydraulic press. The oil was then separated, via centrifuge, from the olive water. It was during this first cold pressing, at room temperature, that the paste yielded its liquid components, which are known as extra-virgin olive oil.

From an old copper spout rushed a cloudy green oil, glinty with golden light from the sun that had come out from behind the clouds. The widow wrung her hands and furrowed her brow; she worried that the absence of chemicals in the growing process would not produce an acceptable, let alone delectable, oil.

I was dying to stick my finger into the spout for a taste, but she had a better idea. She cut off a few slices of thick peasant bread in the way European country women always do, with the knife slicing the loaf toward an ample bosom. She toasted the bread, strewed it on a big plate, and passed the plate under the spout that was now producing a steady spurt of oil. She sprinkled on a pinch of sea salt and offered me a piece as she helped herself to one. We each took a bite, our eyes closed, and we chewed. A big smile stretched across her wrinkled, leathery face. She clasped her hands together and looked heavenward. It was a masterful oil: it was liquid gold.

Olive Oil from Ancestral Spanish Groves

One late-fall day I drove through a pewter-green landscape of hundreds of thousands of olive trees in the world's biggest olive oil–producing area, Andalusia in southern Spain. The land was chalky white from calcium in the soil, and it was dry. I was on my way to visit four brothers who live just north of Granada, near a town called Baena. Their family has produced Nuñez de Prado extra-virgin olive oil since 1795. Unlike many of the neighboring producers in Jaén, the brothers do not target the more commercial end of the olive oil market. They instead make one of Spain's premier condiment extra-virgin olive oils.

The suave and hospitable Nuñez de Prado siblings extended an invitation to experience how the family has, for seven generations, harvested, crushed, and pressed twelve olive varieties into a fine, fruity olive oil. First, they handed me a small wicker basket to strap around my neck. Then off we went into the orchards, to pick, by hand, baskets of green and black olives. I soon learned that black olives are simply green ones that have ripened. My meager contribution was mingled with that of the Spanish pickers and then rushed to the mill for pressing (twenty pounds of olives yield about twelve ounces of oil). There was no time to spare, as olives will ferment and spoil the flavor of the oil if held for more than a day. At the mill, the black and green olives, each with their own flavorful notes, would be crushed by huge Flintstonesque granite stones, turned into a paste, and pressed into a rich, unfiltered, peppery oil that would be ready by lunch, when all of us would taste the result of the morning's labor.

A miller's lunch was laid out in a rustic dining room—partridge and Iberian ham croquettes, Spanish omelets, cauliflower and bone marrow soup, oranges drizzled with honey and olive oil. But from the presses below, the swirling aromas of the fruity, musty oil wafted forth and all I wanted was to taste the source. The distinctive scent alone told me why this oil, which bore hints of flavors from other crops—oranges, almonds, green apples—that grow in the region is considered one of Spain's best.

While we ate, men in white laboratory jackets busily packaged the extra-virgin oil in handsome square bottles topped with red waxed corks. Unlike much of the Spanish oil produced today, Nuñez de Prado is for direct export and not for repackaging in another country.

THE HARVEST

The Press

During the harvest season, there is a flurry of activity, all of it a bit confusing and mysterious, at the small olive presses throughout the Mediterranean. From country to country, region to region, the olive mills whirl into action. Basically, all traditional stone crushers operate the same way: newly harvested olives are washed, deleafed, and crushed, preferably by huge granite stones, into a paste made up of the olive pulp and pits. The paste is then spread on hemp or nylon mats that fit snugly on steel disks stacked one atop the other. Then the disks are wheeled over on a cart to a hydraulic press where extreme pressure is exerted upon them to squeeze out the liquid, which drips from the edges of the disks. The mats allow the oil to drain and at the same time filter out the solid olive matter. The liquid is collected and pumped into a separator, which whisks off the water by centrifugal force and leaves a steady trickle of oil pouring out of its spout.

Many distinguished oils are made by artisanal producers and by wine makers who also happen to have an olive grove. Once olives are harvested, they should be rushed quickly to the press. If left for more than a day or so in sacks or crates, they begin to warm up and ferment, introducing rancidity or the accumulation of off flavors. Some producers have their own presses, but usually oil made on a small scale is pressed, as it has been for hundreds of years, at a communal mill.

Knowledgeable growers demand fastidious procedures at these mills. Cleanliness is critical to the taste of the oil and ultimately to its quality. The mats on which the olive paste is pressed must be properly cleaned or fermentation results, thereby contaminating future pressings. If the presses stop for some reason, the mats must be painstakingly washed so unwanted odors or flavors will not accumulate. Growers also worry that a previous, improperly treated batch of olives (one that may have been infected with olive fly, or left to ferment in a sack) will contaminate a later batch.

In the mills, the wheels grind at a steady, low pitch. The smell of the crushed olives is imposing and intoxicating. In the old days, harnessed animals, such as mules, paced round and round in circles, dragging the wheels through the fresh olives, turning them into a paste. This is called the blood, sweat, and tears press; some olive oil old-timers claim that since oil picks up the flavors of surrounding influences, animal droppings created serious aromatic problems. In some old mills, the repetitive path of these hooved tracks can still be seen. But today, except in parts of Tunisia, much work is done by precision-made machinery.

Fancy estate bottlers often press their olives in their own mills. In Italy, their labels can bear the words "produced and bottled" (*prodotto ed imbottigliato*). In Chianti, little handmade signs announcing *Olio Nuovo* can be seen in shop windows during the harvest season. Small amounts of these artisanal oils are released for export, and buyers await yearly allotments, not unlike wine lovers who look forward each year to Beaujolais *nouveau* (a product, like this olive oil, that does not improve with age).

There are several ways to extract the oil from the olive. One method uses a hydraulic discontinuous press. Here, the press is driven by water under pressure and the liquid that results is transferred to a centrifuge, where separation of the olive oil and olive water occurs. The water is spun off and separated from the oil. The word *discontinuous* means the whole operation is done in batches and does not occur in one continuous motion, as it does in the continuous centrifuge press. With this press, the olive is crushed by stone or, more often, by hammermill. The olive is pressed through a quarter-inch screen, resulting in a mash with three components: olive solids, olive water, and olive oil. After mixing, the mash goes into a decanting or primary centrifuge, where the olive solids are ejected and used for compost or feed for cattle; the olive water and olive oil are left. These components then go into two or more vertical or secondary centrifuges and are separated from each other. It is vital to get the water away from the oil as quickly as possible, as the water will otherwise ferment, causing the oil to change flavor.

A third process is called the sinolea method. Here, the oil-extracting device is equipped with crescent-shaped steel blades that extract oil from ripe olives. The resulting oil drips off the blades and is collected in a trough. An alternative extraction method used by a few producers is called lágrima (Spanish for "tears"). At Almazara, Nuñez de Prado, and Figone in California, the olive paste is layered between esparto-fiber or nylon mats. Teardrops of oil drip from the mats into a trough, where it is collected and lightly filtered before bottling. No exterior pressure is used. A subsequent hydraulic pressing produces a regular olive oil. Neither this method nor the sinolea method exposes the olive to the bruising pressure of the traditional hydraulic press.

On the other end of the spectrum, for the sake of time and expense, the grower might opt for the application of a little hot water during the extraction process, thereby extending the volume of the oil. Florentine writer and food expert Faith Willinger only half-jokingly refers to these hot water–assisted operations as semiscrupulous. In general, enormous pride is taken in cold pressings (no heat applied), first pressings (no water or solvents applied to extend already pressed paste), and stone pressings.

For the most part, artisanal oils are unlike the olive oil most Americans grew up with—the kind that comes in pewter and copper-colored half-gallon cans—the bulk, "workhorse" variety. These oils come from the big industrial presses, impressive with their fancy, state-of-the-art machinery that whirrs and sputters out oils. They are not always really pressed: rather, they are

▲ Hydraulic press

expelled via centrifuge—where the water of the olive, called vegetable water, is spun off from the oil, using a separator—much in the same way cream is separated from milk. Artisanal oils are perfectly good and generally of consistent quality; but they are not oils of grand distinction, and may not be the oils one would want to showcase in a special meal.

Often, particularly in Italy, but in other places, too, these bulk oils are a mixture of oils from various parts of Italy and from Spain, Tunisia, Greece, and even Turkey. Year after year, if you buy a half gallon of one of these everyday oils, you will be neither surprised nor thrilled. There is nothing wrong with an oil that is a blend of disparate oils; many can be very good and they have their place in the kitchen.

The Moment of Truth: Waiting for Oil at the Press

In Chianti, warmly dressed locals arrive at the communal mill in trucks and station wagons with plastic containers or sacks filled with olives and with stainless steel vessels or wicker-covered glass jugs for transporting their oil home. Sometimes there is a little pushing and shoving in the line as these small-scale growers vie for a slot of time at the press. The sounds are high-pitched, the smells are heady, and there's tension in the air. As everyone awaits the result of their hard work and nature's grace, good-humored banter alternates with tentative concern. The farmers often gather in the mill's back room to smoke and drink wine, and to warm their hands over an open fire over which they will also toast bread for dipping into their new oil. The moment of truth arrives as fresh, young, murky oil finally spouts forth. A farmer's olive harvest has the potential to keep the whole family, and even the city relatives, in olive oil for an entire year.

Olive Oil Grades

The grading of olive oil follows a simple hierarchy: extra-virgin olive oil, virgin olive oil, and olive oil. Confusingly, "lite" oils are an attempt to get cooks to buy a rectified oil that is called lite simply because it is light in color and flavor, not in calories or fat.

One of the ways olive oil obtains its grading is on the basis of an acidity evaluation (a chemical test) and then, in the European Community, by a taste evaluation conducted by a panel of highly trained official tasters. California olive oils are not yet graded by tasters.

Extra-virgin olive oils are like fine wines. Their taste and aroma can be distinguished by the seasoned palate, then discussed and dissected. Since the flavors of the olive oils are less debatable and usually less distinguishable than extra-virgins (certainly less expensive), less attention is given to them in this book. Regular olive oil is more like table wine, good in everyday use: good for sautéing, baking, or frying, or whenever high heat is applied in cooking, and good when the distinct flavor of olive oil is not vital to the outcome of a dish.

More attention is given here to extra-virgin olive oils because they are treated differently than olive oils. With the exception of centrifuging and often filtering, extra-virgin oils are untreated.

Extra-Virgin Olive Oil

In the Mediterranean, to qualify for the label "extra-virgin," an olive oil must conform to four criteria: it must be made from the mechanical extraction of olives, be cold pressed, exhibit an acidity level of less than 1 percent, and must have a perfect taste. The taste standard has been created by the International Olive Oil Council. The IOOC is an intergovernmental agency with headquarters in Madrid, Spain, charged with the international coordination of the production, industrialization, and marketing policies of olive oil. (Signees of the United Nations Conference on Olive Oil in 1996 included Algeria, Cyprus, Egypt, the countries of the European Community, Israel, Lebanon, Morocco, Tunisia, Turkey, and the former Yugoslavia. These nations produce more than 98 percent of the world's olive oil.)

After the olives are picked, sorted, and washed, they are crushed and then pressed. That oil becomes a candidate for the extra-virgin grade, provided it passes the acidity and taste tests.

Cold-pressed olive oil refers to oil made from olives crushed with a traditional stone mill or using a discontinuous hydraulic press. No heat or chemicals are administered to extend or alter the oil.

Acidity levels are measured by a simple chemical reaction that records the percentage of the free fatty acid. The best oil has the lowest acidity. As has been noted, extra-virgin olive oil can have no more than 1 percent acidity. It must also display a perceptible fruitiness, and have absolutely no taste or olfactory defects.

The taste test comes after the acidity evaluation. It is the task of highly trained professionals who follow sanctioned criteria to determine whether an oil can be sold as extra-virgin olive oil. Some oils can be chemically adjusted so that they are extra-virgin on paper. Only a chemical test can determine if the oil is extra-virgin.

Olive Oil

Previously called pure olive oil or 100 percent pure olive oil, olive oil is the most widely marketed grade of olive oil and generally costs less than extra-virgin olive oil. It is a combination of extra-virgin oils and refined virgin oils, and must have an acidity level of less than 1.5 percent. It sounds confusing, but since this oil is a blend of oils, its acidity level must meet official standards.

Lite Oil

Light-tasting, light-colored oils that contain only a minute proportion, if any, of virgin oils are sold as lite oils. They are pure rectified oils. They are marketed in such a way as to make people believe that they are purchasing oils low in fat or calories. Actually, lite oils have 125 calories per tablespoon—just like all olive oils, and all fats, for that matter. Olive oil happens to be a good fat—a fat that is said to lower cholesterol levels.

Pomace Oil

The lowest grade of an olive-based oil is pomace oil. It is a blend of virgin oil and refined pomace oil, the latter obtained by using solvents to extract the residual oil left in olive paste after making virgin oil. It is not widely available in the United States at the retail level, but it is used commercially, often for frying and other general cooking uses, as a way to save money.

The Color of Olive Oil

The color palette of most olive-based oils ranges from a pale yellow to a deep cloudy green. It's likely that the latter is an indication the oil is from green, barely ripe olives, perhaps from Tuscany, but not always. An excessive number of leaves may have slipped, inadvertently or not, into the crusher to give a paler, oxidized oil the aura of a better lineage than it actually has. But green is also often an indication of a wonderful, intensely fruity taste and freshness.

Yellow oils usually indicate the olives were picked late in the season when they were black and ripe, producing a sweeter, rounder oil. A lighter color can also signify oxidation, a result of the oil's exposure to sunlight or other light. When this occurs, the oil's delicate aromatic qualities and vitamin E content are usually reduced, and the oil may smell and taste rancid.

23

The Taste of Olive Oil

Mediterraneans grow up appreciating the taste of their local oil, the oil against which all others will always be judged. No other oil will ever quite match their own, have its particular affinity with the foods of the region. When you consume a local oil, explains California organic olive grower Amigo Cantisano, "you are consuming the place, the microclimate, the character of the soil, and, too, the character of the human who produced it, the care with which it has been handled and pressed."

Americans do not bring strong biases to the judging of olive oil. Because olive oil has not been a staple in our cuisine to the extent that it has in Mediterranean countries, we can taste it with an open mind and an unprejudiced tongue.

When you buy olive oil, consider how you will use it, how it will enhance your cooking style. If you are looking for a bold, fruity oil to make a pasta sizzle, a young, peppery Tuscan one might do the trick. Or let's say you have fantastic ripe tomatoes, fresh feta, and good cured olives on hand for a Greek salad. A full-bodied Greek oil would naturally complement such ingredients. Perhaps you desire a hint of olive, but want a background flavor and not actually a condiment. In that case you would need a light, fruity olive oil, perhaps one from Liguria or Provence, one that adds a layer of flavor but does not stand out. When you buy oils for dipping and drizzling you probably want a big-flavored oil, a Tuscan oil perhaps, or a good Spanish oil.

I have noted in most recipes the style of olive oil that I think would be appropriate. There are no strict rules for which type of oil is best—it's all a matter of taste—your taste. One hopes you will have several types of olive oil in a cool, dark spot in your kitchen—a bold, assertive, intensely fruity oil; a mild, medium fruity, background oil (a light but not "lite" oil); and perhaps a lightly fruity, sweet late-harvest oil. Keep a bottle of bulk oil around for heavy-duty uses such as frying, baking, or any high-heat cooking. Experiment, trying out different oils on fish, pasta, salads, and bread. You decide which you prefer.

Official Extra-Virgin Olive Oil Tastings

In the olive oil–producing countries of the Mediterranean, two tests are required to determine the quality of an oil. Once chemical tests have been performed to test for the acidity, then official tasters assemble to determine whether it meets the standards of an extra-virgin. Usually if it has a bad aroma it won't be tasted.

The tasters must follow rules of conduct, commandments really, that have been established by the International Olive Oil Council: They shall not smoke at least thirty minutes before the time set for the test. They shall not use any perfume, cosmetic, or soap whose smell could linger during the test. They shall fast for at least one hour before the tasting is carried out. They must admit to officials if they feel their sense of smell is in any way compromised by illness, or if any persisting psychological stress might prevent concentration on the work at hand.

The process for determining the organoleptic quality (characteristics rating for odor and taste) of an olive oil is based on a specific vocabulary for its sensory analysis. To give an idea of the language olive oil tasters use, here is a list of some official words employed to assess the flavor characteristics of extra-virgin oil: almond, apple, bitter, metallic, muddy sediment, musty-humid, old, pressing mat, pungent, rancid, rough, soapy, sweet, vegetable water, winey-vinegary.

An Olive Oil Tasting at Home

The palate can't remember more than a few oils at a time, so start slow, selecting no more than four or five oils to taste. Keep in mind that extra-virgin olive oils should smell and taste of the fruit from which they are made; they should be fruity, olivey. You might choose a peppery Tuscan oil, a light Ligurian or French oil, a Greek or Spanish oil, perhaps a Californian oil, and possibly even a bulk olive oil for comparison's sake. Keep in mind some of the descriptive words used by official tasters to describe your own experiences.

Pour a little oil into a clean wineglass, cup it between your fingers the way you would a brandy snifter, warming it, then cover the top with your other hand. Swirl it around a few times. Remove your hand and smell the aroma. Then take a tiny sip. Consider the viscosity, how it feels on the roof of your mouth. Suck in air through your teeth so that the flavor is distributed throughout your mouth. Do you like the taste and feel? What flavors are invoked? Are there whispers of almond nuttiness, cucumber, freshly mowed grass, apples, green peppers, or raw artichoke? Try to describe the flavors, then decide if you like them. Before proceeding to the next oil, cleanse your palate with a slice of apple. Bread isn't appropriate for tasting because yeast slightly changes the true taste of the oil and the texture of bread can obscure an oil's viscosity in your mouth.

Try the oils on different foods—slices of boiled potatoes, or celery, perhaps. Determine if an oil enhances your food, or if it is too overpowering on a delicate fish, for example. Might another oil be more or less assertive? Would the olive oil be better on stronger or more subtle foods? Might one oil be so exhilarating that it should only be drizzled on pastas? Is one oil fantastic with bread? Is another best on salads? At the end of the day, if you start to fall in love with olive oil, you will discover you need a few oils in your pantry.

How to Buy Olive Oil

The four enemies of olive oil are age, heat, air, and light. The best way to ensure that whatever olive oil you purchase has not been beset by these foes is to buy from a scrupulous retailer.

The chain supermarket may not be the best place to shop for extra-virgin olive oil, except bulk oils and then only if the turnover is high. Displays are often set up under bright lights, and it's unusual to find a worker passionate enough about olive oil to answer questions for you. You wouldn't go to a supermarket to buy great wines, so don't go to a supermarket to buy great olive oils.

Purchase olive oil from a purveyor who really cares about his or her product. Before selecting an olive oil, ask for an opinion, and look for the harvest date on the bottle, or inquire about the date. No olive oil improves with age, so it should not be more than eighteen months old.

If your area does not have a store that carries a variety of well-kept and documented oils, buy by mail order (see Sources, page 162). It takes only a few days for delivery, and the added shipping expense is worth the quality you will receive. In this case, you'll have to trust the shipper, since you won't be able to taste the oil. Describe how you'll be using the oil and ask for recommendations. The Internet is home to an increasing number of Web sites about olive oil.

Once you determine which source carries oils that consistently have the proper acidity level and dates of harvest, the rest of your decision depends upon style—your style. There is no single best olive oil: it's a matter of personal taste. Try a California oil, a Greek oil, and a Tuscan oil. You'll begin to detect what pleases you, and what to look for.

Many specialty stores offer formal tastings, or will have a few bottles open for tasting upon request. Don't be shy about asking for tastes and advice.

When you travel, taste new and unusual olive oils. Seek out the best oils of a region, buy them, and carry them home or arrange for them to be shipped and waiting for you when you return.

26

Olive Oil Recommendations

Here is a list of extra-virgin oils. It represents my favorites as well as those of olive oil lovers whose palates I respect. I have only included oils that are available in the United States by direct purchase or by mail order (see Sources, page 162; any oil recommended that is available at only a single location is so noted). Although Apulia produces more olive oil than any other Italian region, I have not included a specific Apulian oil because most of what is pressed there is mixed with other oils and sold as bulk Italian oils. Three recommended bulk oils (virgin or plain olive oils) appear at the end of the list.

ITALIAN
TUSCANY
Tenuta del Numerouno
Soft, smooth, lovely, lightly peppery; from the Tuscan-Tyrrhenian seacoast.

Castello di Ama
Rich, smooth, not too peppery; from Siena.

Frescobaldi Laudemio
Classy, sharp, strong, taste of apple—my favorite.

Capezzana
Grassy, herbaeous, good strong finish (pressed by the same method for twelve hundred years).

CENTRAL ITALY
Grandverde Colonna
Olives pressed with lemons.

Olio Agrumato "Medi Terranes" label
Olives pressed with lemons, oranges, or tangerines.

LIGURIA
Roi, Mosto
Unfiltered, light, feathery, delicate bouquet; wrapped in gold foil.

Raineri
Buttery, distinct taste of the olive, yet still delicate.

GARDA
Antonio Bianchi's "I Lecci"
Light, yellow, with a hint of cherries; available only at Zingerman's.

GREEK
Greek Gold Organic
Fruity olive taste; from Mani peninsula.

Kolymvari
Fruity, ripe, grassy taste with golden hues; from Crete.

PORTUGUESE
Quinta da Romaneira
Slightly green, minty, and less fruity than most Spanish oils.

SPANISH
Lérida
Hints of chocolate, slightly peppery, with a golden color; from Catalonia.

L'Estornell
Smooth, bold, rich, slightly almondy, heady; organic from Catalonia.

Nuñez de Prado
Hints of almond, burnt orange, smooth; from Andalusia.

Almazara
Ripe, easy, assertive, almondy, lovely; from Murcia.

CALIFORNIAN
Frantoio Proprietor's Select
Robust, hint of artichoke, light, fruity, buttery.

Lila Jaeger Estate
Complex, grassy, quite delightful.

Harrison Olio d'Oro
Peppery, grassy, full bodied.

McEvoy Ranch
Slightly peppery, robust, Tuscan character.

"O" Olive Oil
Mission olives pressed with Meyer lemons or blood oranges.

Sciabica & Sons Ascalano Oil
Intense fruity, artichoke taste with pepper finish.

B.R. Cohn Sonoma Estate
French style, delicate, hint of citrus, pepper finish.

Davero
Fruity, warm aspects of artichoke and fennel, peppery finish, Tuscan character.

FRENCH
PROVENCE OILS FROM VALLE DES BAUX
M. Bellon's Moulin de Bedarrides
Sweet, buttery, light, tender.

TUNISIAN
Moulins Mahjoub
Elegant, delicate, sweet—like a Provençal oil.

BULK OIL
Colavita
Sasso
Bertolli

The Price of Olive Oil

The five-billion-dollar-a-year olive oil business is just getting hotter and the consumer is exhibiting an increased appetite for the flavor of olive oil, and is finding its perceived health benefits easy to swallow as well.

The prices of small-estate-bottled oils are not reacting to the worldwide shortage in the same way the larger commercial producers of Italian-packed oils are. Why, you might wonder, would Italian olive oil be affected by the Spanish drought? Because not only is Italy a huge consumer of olive oil, but it is also Europe's largest importer.

Most Italian products have a certain cachet these days, and Italian packers know how to capitalize upon this consumer fascination. As long as an oil is packed in Italy, it can be labeled a product of Italy, so the Italian companies benefit. But olive oil producers hoping to upgrade their labeling standards are presently establishing a system similar to the one practiced by wine makers, whereby the source of the oil will be noted on the bottle or can.

A good half-liter bottle of extra-virgin olive oil can cost between eight and thirty dollars—no more expensive than a bottle of wine of corresponding quality.

How to Store Olive Oil

In ancient times, olive oil was stored and transported around the Mediterranean in terra-cotta amphorae, jars with large, oval bodies, narrow cylindrical necks, and two little handles near the mouth. The broad round opening at the top of these graceful vessels permitted easy scooping with a ladle, and their tapered cone-shaped bases allowed them to be stored snugly in clay rings on the ground or in wooden braces aboard ships, where they rested in cool, dark environments.

Even today, it is not uncommon for archaeologists to uncover a date or a stamp of origin on an amphora shard at a dig site. Seals and other trademarks painted or incised on the jars provide important clues that indicate patterns of trade and the movement of Mediterranean civilizations. (On the banks of the Tiber River in Rome, there is a mound of pottery shards that shattered during the loading and unloading of olive oil cargo on the piers of the ancient city, and at the palace of Knossos on Crete, one can still see amphorae from the Minoan period, 1700–1400 B.C.).

The same conditions can be accomplished today by keeping the volatile liquid in a cool, dark place in your house—*never next to the stove*. A wine cellar, a cupboard, or a cool pantry is ideal. Before you bring olive oil home, pay attention to where it has been shelved in the store. Pass up bottles stored under bright lights, for example, or close to a window.

If bought in gallon cans, decant the oil into smaller bottles for easy handling. Red wine bottles are good choices because their dark green color protects the oil from light. Most estate-bottled oils are packaged in tinted glass bottles for this reason. Olive oil can also be stored for short periods in small, disposable plastic water bottles with pull stops. They make for easy measuring and dispensing. Plastic is not a good long-term storage alternative, however, because the oil can absorb its faint but unpleasant properties.

Bottles of olive oil should not be refrigerated. Condensation can occur on the lid and drip water back into the oil, which could spoil the oil's flavor and cause rancidity. Refrigeration also makes the oil cloudy, although it will clarify when it is brought back to room temperature.

Oils mellow and change in intensity as they rest in bulk containers before bottling. Once they are bottled, the flavor can hold or change, and does not improve. They should be used quickly, ideally within a year, or two years at the most. After that, it is downhill.

Olive Oil in California

The olive culture in America is vernal when compared to that of Europe. It began in the mid-1700s, when Spanish Jesuits brought the Mediterranean fruit to Mexico. Toward the end of that century, Franciscan padres from Mexico established the California mission at San Diego de Alcala, where they probably planted the first olive cuttings or seeds. The first oil was most likely pressed at the missions around 1800. Outside of the missions, the Camulos Oil Mill in Ventura, opened in 1871, was probably the first commercial operation. By 1885, olive growers in California were making oils that could compete with the imported European oils. For a while, the state's production increased and prices fell, and then importers drove prices even lower, forcing an eventual decline in California's oil production because of the low costs of subsidized European oils.

In the early 1900s, the olive industry was largely confined to table olives, with oil production relegated to a salvage operation dependent on olives that were too small for curing. By the mid-1900s, other oils—vegetable and seed—gained popularity in the American kitchen mainly because of their comparatively low production costs. In those days, the use of olive oil was virtually nonexistent in the United States, except among first-generation Mediterranean immigrants in large cities and in the surrounding farm areas that fed them.

American interest in olive oil was revitalized in the 1960s and 1970s. Much of the credit goes to the natural-foods movement, which believed in the health benefits of the oil. Then, too, Americans started to travel abroad in greater numbers, and to buy Mediterranean cookbooks and experiment with the region's cuisine, all of which translated into a new demand for olive oil.

Within a few years, Americans were importing about 22 million gallons of olive oil a year. Since California had a climate similar to that of the Mediterranean, and thus perfectly suited to olive growing, it made good sense to resume production. Today, California produces about three hundred thousand gallons of oil each year, although much of it is refined with heat and solvents. Only recently has California begun producing and marketing specialty extra-virgin oils on levels that can begin to compete with oils from Europe.

There were a mere 500 trees in California in 1855; 5,600 in 1876; and half a million at the turn of the century. Nowadays we don't count trees, we count acres, so an exact comparison is impossible. There are, however, about 65,000 acres devoted to olive trees alone. Many of these trees are hundred-year-old Missions, Manzanillos, and Sevillanos, whole orchards that have been brought back to life with careful attention.

Others, such as those owned by the Sciabica family in Modesto, in business since 1936, have been producing extra-virgin and commercial-grade oils all along. The family's fourteen varieties of extra-virgin oils are a familiar sight at farmers' markets around the state. A number of growers who do not have their own presses depend on the Sciabicas for pressing and production expertise. Dan Sciabica, grandson of the founder, says, "In California we don't have huge crops of olives to process all at once. Here we can pick the same variety of olives at different times of the year." He continues, "Americans are used to having a selection, so we release an early- and a late-harvest oil made of the same type of olive. The oil will taste different because one will be from olives that are green and underripe, while the other is from black, sweet, and very ripe olives. They don't usually have that luxury in Europe—their crops are too expansive and need immediate attention."

OLIVE OIL IN CALIFORNIA

Olives and grapevines have co-existed in the Mediterranean for millennia. Here, an increasing number of California wine growers are becoming olive oil producers, too. Many now have new trees on their property, or are restoring abandoned orchards. One such grower is Lila Jaeger, whom many of her peers refer to as the domestic visionary of the extra-virgin olive oil movement in California. Jaeger's family's wine business, Rutherford Hills, in the Napa Valley, began getting well-deserved attention, and needed to develop more space to cope with visitors. Jaeger cleared a plot of land, only to uncover a hundred-year-old olive orchard. The trees sprang back to life with a minimum of attention. Her first harvest was pressed at Sciabica, and resulted in an oil that showed very well in a blind tasting. That was all the encouragement she needed to proceed with confidence. Each year since, she has experimented with the time of harvest, and is now delighted with the results of picking between November 15 and 25. A batch of French varietals has recently been added to her California crop of Spanish olives.

Few estate growers are making significant money at this luxury-farming enterprise, but as a group, and independently, they take themselves seriously. Members of the California Olive Oil Council are helpful and supportive of one another, and many maintain staunch opinions about time of harvest and method of pressing. Options for making olive oil have opened up in recent years beyond the big mills of the Sciabicas, Golden Eagle, Stonehouse, and the Orland Olive Oil Company.

Jill Harrison and her husband, Chris Willis, of Harrison Vineyards, started to crush their Olio d'Oro a few years ago in a small discontinuous press with a stone crusher. Their hand-painted bottles filled with a deep green oil made from a blend of olives is now familiar at tastings and on shelves of specialty stores throughout the country.

Chef-owner Michael Chiarello of Tra Vigne Restaurant, who is also a partner in Napa Valley Kitchens, has been producing olive oils on a grand scale, ones quite different from those of his peers. Under the label Consorzio, he has popularized infused oils (mild oils steeped with peppers, basil, and garlic). But he also has bought land in Orland, one of the olive capitals of California, for a new production enterprise, and has released an oil, from olives harvested in his orchard, specifically for cooking.

Bruce Cohn (B. R. Cohn), former manager of the Doobie Brothers, and California Olive Oil Council president Greg Reisinger make oil from 125-year-old trees at Olive Hill, a former stagecoach stop in the Valley of the Moon, near Glen Ellen. They produce oils, like Jaeger, from abandoned, restored orchards, and their labels include a French estate Picholine and an extra-virgin in fancy numbered edition bottles with etched glass.

Few people are as well versed in the vernacular of olive oil from an Italian and Californian point of view as Roberto Zecca, who for five years produced a very fine oil on his Tuscan estate. He moved to California from his Chianti farm, and built a restaurant called Frantoio (Italian for "mill"), complete with a state-of-the-art Pieralisi discontinuous hydraulic olive oil press that runs as a separate enterprise within the restaurant. Zecca buys olives and presses his own oils under the Frantoio label. He also presses for a few growers, who are drawn to his specific production process and traditional stone crusher. It is an old-fashioned and expensive method of pressing olives, and it is labor-intensive.

California growers have access to olives long cultivated for eating, and, until recently, only incidentally pressed into olive oil. But in the past decade, careful growing, harvesting, and pressing procedures have resulted in a number of premium-quality oils pressed from table olives. Other than those names already mentioned, others to watch for are Evo, Figone, Pascarelli & Jones, Stutz, Katz & Co., Vine Hill Farms, Round Pond, and Sadec Organic Oil. Every year the list grows, and the oils improve.

Several growers, led by former newspaper chair Nan Tucker McEvoy and Silicon Valley tycoon Ridgely Evers, have imported bare-root olive trees from Tuscany. Both have been rewarded with success because of mindful planting, harvesting, and pressing procedures, and a climate similar to Tuscany. The first commercial olive orchard in Marin County, the McEvoy Ranch hired Italian enologist and agronomist Dr. Maurizio Castelli to consult with the selection of olive varieties that include Leccino, Frantoio, Maurino, Pendolino, and smaller numbers of Picholine. He offers advice on cultivation through all stages of planting, including the propagation program at McEvoy's 550-acre ranch near Petaluma. While delighted with results from the first successful stone pressing—performed at Frantoio in Mill Valley—McEvoy is installing her own equipment for the sinolea system (see page 21).

Evers chose to emulate his favorite Italian oil from Fattoria Mansi-Bernardini, near Lucca, and has, in Healdsburg, California, carefully planted thirty-five hundred Tuscan olive trees (Leccino, Frantoio, Maurino, and Pendolino). He is turning out wonderful oil and lists both the date of harvest, the varietal mix, and the acidity level on his label.

A California Olive Oil Tasting

Six little plastic cups filled with extra-virgin oil were set in front of each seat in an amphitheater classroom at the Culinary Institute of America in St. Helena, California. Members of the California Olive Oil Council were gathered for a blind tasting of five California oils and, for comparison's sake, one wildcat Italian oil. On an extraordinarily fine May day, well after the olive harvest had ended, the mellowed, settled, California oils had been poured into fancy estate bottles. It was time to taste and learn about these olive oils and others like them—olive oils that are opening the latest chapter of California's agrarian and culinary history.

Before the blind tasting, members were invited to sample oils in an open tasting, where the oils were poured from shapely bottles with artistic, well-identified labels. The selection included olive oil from twenty-five of the forty-odd producers in California, in colors ranging from bright acid green to pale golden yellow. They reflected the colors of the Napa, Sonoma, and Central valleys and the Sierra foothills—the areas where olives grow in the Golden State.

Leading the tasting was internationally known wine and olive oil expert Darrell Corti of Corti Brothers, the venerable Sacramento family grocery. Some local olive oil producers were concerned because Corti has, in the past, been critical of California oils, while others feel he keeps everyone on their toes. He favors well-established Mediterranean oils, but his palate is legendary, and everybody is anxious to learn. California growers and producers are poised and ready for growth. The industry is now in a position equivalent to that of the state's burgeoning wine industry in the early 1960s.

The tasting procedure was an educational exercise. Members were shown how to taste oils properly, and how to record their findings. Adjusting one's palate to olive oil is a very subtle process. There are many nuances to consider and, let's face it, tasting oil straight is not as romantic as tasting wine.

Official olive oil tasters do not exist in California as they do in many of the olive oil–producing countries that belong to the International Olive Oil Council. Those countries are regulated by strict sanctions; America, at present, is not. In fact, producers of extra-virgin olive oil in California are on the honor system to produce extra-virgin oils with all the conscientiousness of their European counterparts.

Olive Oil in the Kitchen

Baking with Olive Oil

The use of olive oil in baking dramatically cuts the cholesterol and saturated-fat content of a sweet or bread. It produces lighter-tasting baked goods and allows the flavor of the other ingredients to shine. I have had success with olive oil in baking flat breads, pizzas, brownies, biscotti, citrus cake, breakfast breads, quick breads, and focaccia. You need less olive oil than other fats in baking.

Use the following conversion chart as a general guide for adapting recipes.

BUTTER	OLIVE OIL
1 teaspoon	3/4 teaspoon
1 tablespoon	2 1/4 teaspoons
2 tablespoons	1/2 tablespoon
1/4 cup	3 tablespoons
1/3 cup	1/4 cup
1/2 cup	1/4 cup plus 2 tablespoons
2/3 cup	1/2 cup
3/4 cup	1/2 cup plus 1 tablespoon
1 cup	3/4 cup

Deep-Frying with Olive Oil

Frying is one of the world's oldest cooking methods and a way of life in the Mediterranean. Italians love to fry *crocchette di riso* (rice croquettes), *fritto misto di mare* (assorted seafood), fritters, zucchini blossoms, sardines, and anchovies, and even fresh herbs such as parsley and sage. *Briks* and *braewats*, small pastry envelopes filled with spicy savories, are popular in Morocco and Tunisia. In Greece, fried cheese is drizzled with honey and served for dessert (see page 159). Greeks also fry all kinds of fish, pastry ribbons, cheese, bread, and even snails with peppers. In Spain, a variety of fried foods are eaten from breakfast to bedtime, including *churros*, *buñuelos*, cheese balls, and assorted fish. In the south of France cooks fry eggplant, whitebait, and beignets.

A small slicing machine imported from Japan or a French mandoline will turn any firm vegetable into paper-thin shapes ideal for frying. Chips made from vegetables such as yams, carrots, beets, zucchini, artichokes, fennel, onions, turnips, and russet potatoes are all lovely fried in olive oil.

WHAT KIND OF OIL IS BEST FOR FRYING?
Since the application of heat removes the fruity character of olive oil, it does not make sense to fry with an expensive one. Many chefs and home cooks use virgin oil or olive oil for frying. Unlike extra-virgin, these oils impart little or no flavor to foods, and they remain stable at fairly high temperatures because of their low oleic acid and antioxidant properties. Frying in olive oil seals in the moisture, simultaneously creating a crispy crust, with the flavor of olive oil.

Southern frying expert "Hoppin'" John Taylor uses generic (bulk) extra-virgin olive oil for deep-frying because "it absolutely tastes better, and I trust the processing of extra-virgin olive oil over the lesser grade oils." He fries in deep, cast-iron pots because they hold heat well, and uses a thermometer to test the oil temperature. "I even fry chicken and whole Cornish game hens in olive oil, and that's saying a lot for a southerner."

WHAT HAPPENS WHEN YOU FRY WITH OLIVE OIL?

Look at how much oil is left in a pan when you sauté, and then take a look at what remains in the pan after you deep-fry. When you sauté, very little oil remains because it's been absorbed into the food. But frying with olive oil is a dry-cooking process, and if it's done right, no oil will penetrate the food.

During frying, cooking fat replaces part of the water naturally in the food. In fact, what makes fried food taste good is that this exchange actually enhances its flavor. Sixty percent of a food's moisture content must evaporate before the olive oil begins to penetrate; other fats insinuate themselves more quickly. Therefore, frying in olive oil renders food less greasy, more crunchy, with lower fat content, and fewer calories than food fried in other fats.

The formation of a crust on deep-fried foods not only creates crunchiness, but also prevents further penetration of oil. Plus, since food fried in olive oil does not remain in the pan for long, vitamins do not have time to evaporate. In fact, during deep-frying, water-soluble vitamins are not leached out to the extent they are when foods are boiled in water.

Tips for Frying with Olive Oil

- Use a deep-fat fryer with the thermostat set to 350 to 365 degrees F, or clip a thermometer onto the side of a nonelectric pan.

- Make sure you fry in oil at least $2^1/2$ inches deep and heat the oil slowly.

- Do not add too many pieces of food to the oil at once, or the temperature of the oil will drop and you won't get crispy, golden brown results.

- If more oil is needed, add it to the hot oil and wait for the temperature to return to the original temperature before proceeding.

- Lift food out with spring-loaded tongs (slotted spoons hold oil).

- Salt draws water out of fried food, rendering it soggy; let diners salt their own portions.

- Drain fried foods on wire racks placed over paper towels. Foods drained directly on paper towels reabsorb the drained oil.

- When you have finished frying, clarify the oil by frying a piece of bread, a strip of lemon peel, or a slice of potato in it.

- Once cooled, strain the oil through cheesecloth or a paper coffee filter, then store in a refrigerator. Do not use the same oil more than three times, although olive oil experts say that between seven and ten times is safe. This is an exception to the recommendation not to store olive oil in the refrigerator.

Starters & Soups

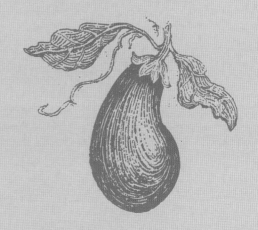

Brandade of Salt Cod

Serves 8 to 10

This Provençal dish is usually served as a first course, but it can be eaten as a light supper as well, accompanied with a green salad. Buy skinned and boned salt cod, and be prepared to soak it for at least a day or a day and a half in repeated changes of cold water before cooking. Since the flavors are strong and "of the sea," use a mild French extra-virgin or a good bulk extra-virgin olive oil. The finished brandade should have the appearance of creamy mashed potatoes.

1 pound skinless, boneless salt cod

2 heads garlic, loose outer papery sheaths removed

¹/₂ cup plus 4 tablespoons extra-virgin olive oil

3 russet potatoes, peeled and quartered

1 teaspoon white pepper

¹/₂ cup milk

Toasted baguette or French bread slices brushed with extra-virgin olive oil

Put the salt cod in a large bowl with cold water to cover. Refrigerate for 24 to 36 hours, changing the water at least 4 times.

When you are ready to assemble the dish, preheat the oven to 350 degrees F. Cut off the pointed tops of the garlic heads. In an ovenproof cast-iron skillet over medium heat, warm 2 tablespoons of the olive oil for 1 minute. Place the garlic heads cut side down in the olive oil and brown lightly for 2 to 3 minutes. Turn the garlic heads cut side up and drizzle 2 more tablespoons of oil over the tops. Cover the skillet with aluminum foil and place in the oven. (Or transfer to a baking dish, cover, and place in the oven.) Roast until the cloves are soft enough to squeeze free easily of their papery sheaths, 45 minutes to 1 hour. When cool enough to handle, squeeze the roasted cloves from their papery sheaths and set aside.

Transfer the salt cod and its last batch of soaking water to a large saucepan and bring to a boil. Reduce the heat to medium-low, and simmer until tender when pierced with a knife, 10 to 15 minutes. Do not overcook or it will toughen.

Using a slotted spatula or a slotted spoon, remove the cod to a bowl. When cool enough to handle, break it up with your fingers, being careful to remove any stray bones or pieces of skin. Meanwhile, add the potatoes to the same water, bring to a slow, rolling boil, and cook over medium heat until tender, 15 to 20 minutes. Drain.

Take the bowl containing the cod, add the squeezed garlic, potatoes, pepper, and milk, and beat with an electric mixer for a few seconds until the ingredients are integrated. Drizzle in all but 2 tablespoons of the remaining ¹/₂ cup olive oil and whip until the mixture is creamy.

Transfer the *brandade* to a shallow oval dish and drizzle the reserved olive oil over the top. Serve warm with the olive oil–brushed bread slices.

38

Eggplant Tonnato

Serves 4 to 6

At a baroque villa in the center of the ancient town of Lecce in Apulia on Italy's southeastern tip, I was part of a culinary group that came together for a lavish twenty-five-course dinner. It was a meal a merchant might have served long ago to show off his wealth. Of all the dishes we had, this was my favorite. It is a variation on vitello tonnato, the famed Lombardian antipasto made with veal. The eggplant can be grilled on an outdoor or stove-top grill or cooked in a cast-iron frying pan over high heat.

1 medium to large eggplant, sliced into thin rounds

Salt

Extra-virgin olive oil for brushing eggplant slices

2 cans (3 1/4 ounces each) Italian tuna in olive oil, broken up but not drained

5 tablespoons salt-cured capers, rinsed and drained

1 tablespoon fresh lemon juice

Grated zest of 1 lemon

2 oil-packed anchovy fillets, rinsed and chopped

1/4 cup extra-virgin olive oil

2 cloves garlic, crushed

Freshly cracked pepper to taste

A few fresh Italian parsley sprigs

Line a large colander with the eggplant slices, sprinkling each layer liberally with salt. Top with a heavy bowl to weight down the slices. After about 30 minutes, rinse the slices under cold running water. Pat dry.

Brush each eggplant slice with a little olive oil. Grill over a charcoal fire, in a cast-iron frying pan over high heat, or on a stove-top grill until soft and nicely browned, a few minutes on each side. Brush again with olive oil after turning. Set aside on a rack and allow to cool.

In a blender or food processor, combine the tuna, 3 tablespoons of the capers, lemon juice, lemon zest, anchovies, the 1/4 cup olive oil, garlic, and pepper. Blend until smooth. Transfer to a bowl.

Lay the grilled eggplant slices on a platter. Put a dab of the tuna mixture, about 1 tablespoon, on each slice and roll up. Secure with toothpicks if necessary, although they will probably hold together on their own. Put a parsley leaf at the end of each roll. Arrange the rolls on the platter. If the end rounds of the eggplant are too small to roll, simply put a dab of the tuna mixture on top with a parsley leaf, as if putting cheese on a cracker. Sprinkle with the remaining 2 tablespoons capers. Serve at room temperature.

Artichokes Angelo

Serves 4 to 6

One night I was at a dinner party in San Francisco at Angelo Garro's forge, where he produces extraordinary artisanal metal works. The guests, who included local chefs, were all warming their hands around a huge oil-drum barbecue while a small boar rotated over the hot coals. As the beast crackled and darkened, the discussion turned to the foods of spring, as the new season was just days away. Lovely little artichokes had been seen by everyone at the farmers' market that morning, and they all had strong opinions about how to prepare them. I had to confess that I never quite knew what to do with them, so Angelo invited me over a few days later to help him trim and marinate a case of baby artichokes.

2 lemons

24 baby artichokes,
   about 2 ounces each

2 cups water

2 cups red wine vinegar

4 cloves garlic, finely chopped

20 fresh mint leaves, cut into
   julienne strips

⅓ to ½ cup extra-virgin olive
   oil

Salt and freshly ground pepper
   to taste

Fill a bowl with water and squeeze in the juice from the lemons, then throw in the lemon halves.

Select green, firm artichokes without any black spots. Remove at least three layers of outer leaves to reach the light green interior leaves. Working with 1 artichoke at a time, trim off the dark spot where the artichoke was attached to the bush and the pointed top 1 inch of the leaves. Cut in half lengthwise (or in quarters if you have had to use larger artichokes). As they are cut, slip them into the lemon water.

In a large saucepan bring the 2 cups each water and vinegar to a boil. Drain the artichokes, discarding the lemon halves. Add them to the saucepan and bring back to a boil. Boil until tender, 10 to 15 minutes. Drain in a large colander for 30 minutes so that most of the moisture is gone.

In a ceramic bowl, combine the garlic, mint, olive oil, and salt and pepper. Toss with the drained artichokes. They will have a fuller, more delightful flavor if served later in the day, or after 24 hours of marinating, if you can wait that long. The artichokes can also be stored in a jar in the refrigerator, in olive oil to cover, for a few weeks. Bring to room temperature before serving.

Bagna Cauda

Serves 6 to 8

Bagna cauda, literally "hot bath," is a sixteenth-century Piedmontese dish that was traditionally eaten to celebrate the end of the grape harvest and the new wine for the coming year. Since Piedmont is landlocked, it is odd that its inhabitants would favor anchovies in this dish. "But," food writer Janet Fletcher says, "in earlier times, traders from the Ligurian coast would climb the fertile hills to swap salt and salted fish for garlic and vegetables in Piedmont."

Customarily, *bagna cauda* is served as a dip in a *fornelletto*, a little terra-cotta bowl kept warm over a candle, with assorted trimmed vegetables and breadsticks for dipping. Some Italians scramble an egg into the *fornelletto* when most of the dip is gone, and then shave a little white truffle on top.

The olive oil will be overpowered by the garlic and anchovies, so I do not suggest using your favorite oil, but a good, basic one.

1 head garlic

1½ cups extra-virgin olive oil

10 salt-cured anchovies, filleted and rinsed, or 20 oil-packed anchovy fillets, rinsed

Freshly cracked pepper to taste

Assorted trimmed vegetables (see note) and breadsticks

Separate the head of garlic into cloves, peel, and chop. In a heavy cast-iron skillet, combine the olive oil and garlic. Place over very low heat and cook until the garlic is translucent, 30 to 45 minutes. Watch very carefully; the garlic must not brown or the sauce will be bitter.

Add the anchovies to the garlic-oil mixture and stir with a wooden spoon until the anchovies melt, about 15 minutes. Add pepper to taste. Transfer to individually warmed pots or keep warm on a hot plate. The sauce should remain hot, but should not boil. Serve with vegetables and breadsticks for dipping.

Note: Assorted vegetables can include artichokes, steamed asparagus, steamed Brussels sprouts, cardoons, carrots, cauliflower, celery, chard, endive, fennel, leeks, mushrooms, yellow or red bell peppers, boiled potatoes, radicchio, and radishes.

Foods Conserved in Olive Oil

Olive oil has been used to conserve vegetables, fish, and meat in Mediterranean countries for millennia. In Italy, the method is called *sott'olio*, "under oil." The idea is to cover food with oil in a jar so that no oxygen reaches it. If you plan to serve one of the following foods, such as the slivered artichokes, right away, cover completely with olive oil.

Use only the best quality extra-virgin oil, as its taste will permeate the food being conserved. You'll also need very clean screw-top or spring-top jars. If possible, wash them in a dishwasher and fill them while they are still hot from the drying cycle, making sure there are no water droplets on the glass.

The ingredients must be absolutely dry before adding them to the oil because water can cause fermentation, as can air bubbles. If the oil has a good flavor after you have finished the jar of conserves, use it to flavor a pasta or salad. Immerse the ingredients completely in the oil and let it stand for at least a half hour before serving. When you eat a portion, always be certain that what remains in the jar is covered with oil, adding fresh oil to the jar as needed.

Although in the past the oil sufficed as a preservative, provided the jars were stored in a cool, dark spot, today, for safety's sake, it is best to refrigerate the jars and then bring the contents slowly back to room temperature before serving. Check stored jars for bubbling or domed lids, which indicate fermentation, and throw out any that you suspect.

43

Kalamata Olives with Orange Rind

Makes about 1 $^1/_2$ cups

Black, round on one end, and slightly pointed on the other, Kalamata olives are imported from Greece, usually immersed in a brine. Preparing them as described here results in a beautiful jar of black olives laced with strips of orange rind and garlic cloves. They can be stored in the refrigerator for months.

$^1/_2$ pound Kalamata olives

Extra-virgin olive oil to cover

Rind of 1 orange, cut into strips about $^1/_4$ inch wide and 1 inch long

2 cloves garlic, slivered

Rinse the olives in cool water, then turn them out onto a kitchen towel and pat dry. Place in a bowl and add the olive oil, orange rind, and garlic. Toss to mix evenly and store in a clean 1 $^1/_2$-cup jar until ready to use. To serve, remove the olives with tongs so that they are not dripping with oil.

Roasted Sweet Peppers with Garlic

Makes about 3 cups

Equal amounts of yellow and red peppers can be used in place of all red. Serve on toast with a few capers and anchovies, or serve as an antipasto with a little chopped fresh basil, Italian parsley, or oregano.

4 pounds red bell peppers (about 8 medium)

1 bay leaf

6 to 8 peppercorns

4 to 6 cloves garlic, thinly sliced

Salt

Mild extra-virgin olive oil, preferably French or Italian, to cover

Roast the peppers over the flame of a gas stove or in a broiler until the skins are blackened and blistered. Put them in a bowl and cover snugly with a kitchen towel. When cool enough to handle, peel off the skin, cut in half lengthwise and remove and discard the stem and seeds. Slice lengthwise into strips about $^1/_2$ inch wide.

Pack the pepper strips into a clean 1 $^1/_2$-pint jar, sliding the bay leaf along the wall of the jar and sprinkling the peppercorns, garlic, and a little salt throughout. Pour in olive oil to cover completely. Cover tightly and store for up to 1 week in the refrigerator.

44

Slivered Raw Artichokes with Pecorino

Makes 2 to 3 cups

San Francisco chef Scott Warner serves these little shaved artichokes with French olive oil and shards of pecorino at Reed Hearon's restaurant, Rose Pistola. I have two orders every time I go.

24 baby artichokes, about 2 ounces each

Juice of 2 lemons

Extra-virgin olive oil to coat or to cover

Salt and freshly ground pepper to taste

¼ pound pecorino cheese

Fill a bowl with water and squeeze in the juice from 1 lemon, then throw in the lemon halves.

Select green, firm artichokes without any black spots. Remove at least three layers of outer leaves to reach the light green interior leaves. Working with 1 artichoke at a time, trim off the dark spot where the artichoke was attached to the bush and the pointed top 1 inch of the leaves. Cut the trimmed artichoke in half lengthwise, and lay flat side down. Using a very sharp knife (or a mandoline), slice the artichoke lengthwise as thinly as possible. Slip the slices into the lemon water. When all the artichokes are done, drain, pat dry, and place in a bowl. Squeeze the juice of the remaining lemon over the artichokes and add enough olive oil to coat. Season with salt and pepper and toss to coat evenly.

The artichokes are best served immediately, as they start to brown if exposed to the air for more than 15 minutes. (If you decide to take them on a picnic, prepare them that day and store them in a jar, completely covered with olive oil.) Turn them onto a serving platter and, using a vegetable peeler, shave curls of pecorino cheese over the top. Serve at once.

Feta Cheese with Oregano

Makes about 2 cups

Combine these marinated feta cubes with tomatoes for a Greek salad or with Kalamata olives for an appetizer, or simply serve on top of bread.

1 pound feta cheese

½ red onion, very thinly sliced

1 tablespoon dried oregano

1 teaspoon black, red, or green peppercorns

Extra-virgin olive oil, preferably Greek, to cover

Drain the feta cheese well and pat dry with paper towels. Cut into 1-inch cubes. Do not worry if the cheese crumbles slightly. Pack the feta cubes into a clean 1-pint jar, layering them with the onion slices, oregano, and peppercorns. Pour in olive oil to cover completely. Cover tightly and store in the refrigerator for up to 1 week.

45

Fennel Slices with Chilies
Makes about 1 1/2 cups

These crunchy slices of fennel are best if eaten immediately. Like artichoke hearts, they start to brown once they are cut. If you take them in a jar on a picnic, make them that day.

2 fennel bulbs

1/2 teaspoon Dijon mustard

Splash of red wine vinegar

Salt and freshly ground pepper to taste

Extra-virgin olive oil to coat or to cover

2 small dried red chilies

Trim off the feathery tops and stalks from the fennel bulbs, reserving a few tops. Cut off any bruised leaves from the bulbs, cut in half lengthwise, core, and then cut into paper-thin slices.

In a small bowl, mix together the mustard, vinegar, salt and pepper. Toss with the fennel slices. Pour enough olive oil over the fennel slices to coat and toss again. Scatter a few feathery fennel tops and the chilies on top and serve.

If you do not plan to eat the sliced fennel immediately, pack it into a clean 1-pint jar, sliding the chilies along the walls of the jar and scattering a few feathery fennel tops throughout. Pour in olive oil to cover completely.

Sun-dried Tomatoes with Anchovies, Capers, and Fennel Seeds
Makes 10 "sandwiches"

This recipe, inspired by one in *Honey from a Weed* by Patience Grey, offers an interesting twist on the ubiquitous sun-dried tomato.

5 oil-packed anchovy fillets, rinsed, dried, and cut in half crosswise

3 tablespoons salted capers, rinsed and patted dry

1 tablespoon fennel seeds

20 dry-packed sun-dried tomatoes

1 bay leaf

Extra-virgin olive oil to cover

Place a piece of anchovy, a few capers, and a few fennel seeds in each of 10 sun-dried tomatoes. Top with another dried tomato and press together firmly as if making a sandwich. Place in a clean, small, stout jar, stacking them tightly. Slide the bay leaf along the wall of the jar, pour in olive oil to cover, and cap tightly. The dried tomatoes need a day to soften in the oil before using. Store in the refrigerator for up to 1 week. Bring to room temperature before serving.

46

Bocconcini with Basil

Makes about 2 cups

Bocconcini are small balls of fresh mozzarella made, preferably, with water buffalo milk. Use your best Tuscan extra-virgin oil. Serve with very ripe tomatoes or as an antipasto.

½ pound *bocconcini*

6 to 8 fresh basil leaves

1 teaspoon black, red, or green peppercorns, or a mixture

1 small dried red chili pepper

Extra-virgin olive oil, preferably Tuscan, to cover

Pat the *bocconcini* dry with paper towels. Pack the cheeses into a clean 1-pint jar, scattering in among them the basil leaves, peppercorns, and chili pepper so that the seasonings are visible through the walls of the jar. Add olive oil to cover completely, cover tightly, and store in the refrigerator for up to 1 week.

Note: Goat cheese rounds can be marinated with the same ingredients for 1 hour or more before serving. Store in the refrigerator for up to 3 days.

In the rolling coastal hills near the town of Petaluma, Nan Tucker McEvoy, a relative newcomer to the olive oil scene in Northern California, has planted thousands of imported Italian olive trees. She has retained as her consultant Maurizio Castelli, who oversees the wine and olive oil production at Badia a Coltibuono, owned by Piero Stucchi-Prinetti and his wife, well-known Italian cook Lorenza de' Medici.

I brought a picnic for McEvoy and a few friends one stormy spring day. We ate an array of conserved-in-olive-oil treats with crusty country bread. Each conserve was made with a different olive oil, and everyone had to guess which one was made with the McEvoy oil. Nan McEvoy guessed correctly—the jar with the roasted sweet peppers and garlic.

47

Oil-cured Fish
Makes 1 to 1½ cups

At Rose Pistola restaurant, San Francisco chef Reed Hearon often presents a lovely array of oil-cured fish—swordfish, salmon, sardines, anchovies—alongside slivered artichokes (see page 45) or fresh favas with pecorino, all of them displayed in graceful oval serving dishes.

In the Mediterranean, fish cured in oil is stored in jars or earthenware crocks in cool, dark areas. Because most houses in the United States no longer have cool pantries suitable for keeping the fish, I recommend storing it in the refrigerator. If you are taking the fish on a picnic, remove the jar from the refrigerator and allow the oil to uncloud slowly as you drive to your destination. Use only the highest-quality, freshest fish for this recipe.

½ pound swordfish, salmon, or tuna fillet or cleaned whole anchovies or sardines

¼ cup fresh lemon juice

¼ cup dry white wine

Salt

Mild extra-virgin olive oil to cover

2 or 3 paper-thin slices white onion or shallot

Freshly ground pepper to taste

Thinly slice the fish fillets into slender strips about 2 inches long. If you are using anchovies or sardines, fillet them and cut in half lengthwise. Do not slice.

In a measuring pitcher, combine the lemon juice and white wine with enough salt to make the mixture pleasantly salty. Place the fish in a single layer in a shallow dish and pour the wine mixture over it. Allow to rest until the fish turns almost opaque, 30 minutes to 1 hour. The lemon juice and the wine will "cook" the fish slightly.

Line a wire rack with a clean kitchen towel. Remove the fish from the marinade, place on the towel-covered rack, and top with a second towel. Allow to drain for 10 minutes, then press down on the towels to remove any moisture. Transfer to a serving platter and add olive oil just to cover. Sprinkle with the onion or shallot slices and pepper and serve. Or pack the fish and the onion or shallot into a clean 1- to 1½-cup jar, add olive oil to cover completely, and store in the refrigerator for up to 2 days.

48

Pinzimonio

I ate a dish of simple raw vegetables and olive oil at Trattoria Vecchia Lugano on the shores of Lake Garda, after touring some of the old olive presses in the region. The oil of the Veneto is yellow and mild. It is hard to find in the United States, except at Zingerman's in Ann Arbor, Michigan (see Sources, page 162), so another extra-virgin oil might have to do until you can send away for it or pick up some on your next trip to northern Italy.

The restaurant assembled glass buckets filled with ice and cut raw vegetables arranged like bouquets of flowers. The buckets were placed along the length of a long dining table, each with its own dish of olive oil seasoned with salt and pepper. This dish, called *pinzimonio*, is sometimes served between courses—an Italian custom for refreshing the palate.

Select an assortment of very fresh, flawless vegetables, and trim and cut them into long, elegant slices or strips for ease of dipping. Among the possibilities are fennel, Belgian endive, radicchio, carrots, celery, English cucumber, whole radishes, and red, yellow, and orange bell peppers.

Arrange the vegetables in tall containers. Place a shallow dish of extra-virgin olive oil mixed with sea salt and freshly cracked pepper alongside each container.

Toasts with Olive Oil

Serves 6 to 8

One early afternoon during the olive harvest in Radda-in-Chianti, in Tuscany, forty or fifty rosy-cheeked men in navy blue jackets were finishing lunch in the town's tiny cafe. They were preparing to return to the olive orchards, when I entered with two other American women, hungry and cold. At first we were a bit startled by all the attention we received. But while we were waiting for our drinks to be served, the encounter became fun and lively as we bantered back and forth with our new acquaintances about what we should eat. It was settled. We'd have *fettuntas*, grilled toast rubbed with a clove of garlic and drizzled with *olio nuovo*, new oil from the press just down the road in Volpaia. We also had *crostini* with the end of the season's tomatoes.

In Tuscany, *crostini di fegatini*—made with chicken livers—are favorites. But many other toppings are possible as well, including a few leaves of arugula tossed with vinegar, olive oil, salt, and pepper, or creamy puréed white beans drizzled with a good, green extra-virgin olive oil (page 23).

In Spain, the first thing a baby eats after mother's milk is *pa amb tomaquet,* bread rubbed with garlic and tomato, then drizzled with olive oil. The Catalonian dish is simple and delightful: Toast thick slices of country-style bread, rub with garlic cloves, and then cup a tomato in your palm and rub it on the bread so that only the skin remains in your hand. Drizzle Spanish olive oil on top and season with salt and pepper. Eat as is, or add a few pieces of anchovy or chorizo.

1 large loaf Italian country-style bread, thickly sliced

Garlic cloves

Best, freshest extra-virgin olive oil available, preferably Tuscan

Grill or toast the bread slices, then rub with a clove of garlic until it almost melts into the bread. Drizzle with olive oil.

Variations: Top the toast with chopped fresh tomatoes, salt and pepper, and ribbons of fresh basil; anchovies and fresh Italian parsley leaves; roasted bell peppers in olive oil; or olive purée or eggplant purée.

Double-decker Israeli Cream Cheese Cake
with Sesame and Oregano
Serves 8

For years, I had been running into the same woman at the farmers' market. I surmised she cooked like I did since we always gravitated to the same vendors. One day, Tallia Hillel introduced herself and we talked about two of our shared interests—food and olive oil. When we started discussing recipes, she gave me this Israeli one. It would be ideal, of course, with Israeli olive oil, but it is only just beginning to appear in the United States. Any fine, full-flavored, extra-virgin oil will work well, however. Since the cheese is mild, the oil is the element that makes the dish come alive.

$^1/_3$ cup sesame seeds

$1^1/_2$ tablespoons dried oregano

Pinch of salt

1 pound cream cheese, at room temperature

3 tablespoons extra-virgin olive oil, preferably Israeli or Greek

Crackers or toasted pita triangles

In a small frying pan over medium heat, heat the sesame seeds for 1 minute to warm them and release their flavor. Remove from the heat before they begin to pop. Pour into a small bowl and mix in the oregano and salt.

Divide the cream cheese in half. Using your hands, roll each half into a ball, then flatten each ball into a disk about $1^1/_2$ inches thick. On a serving plate, place one flattened ball, sprinkle with half of the sesame seed mixture, and drizzle with 1 tablespoon of the olive oil. Put the other flattened ball on top and distribute the rest of the sesame seed mixture over the surface. Drizzle the remaining olive oil over the top. Serve with crackers or pita triangles.

Greek Roasted Red Pepper and Feta Dip

Makes about 2 cups

Upon arriving in Athens after a long flight, I ended up at Daphne's Restaurant. *Htipiti,* a mixture of peppers and feta, was the first thing I ate. Its psychedelic color was jarring, but the flavor was soothing, and after a few bites, my jet lag was long gone. It can be eaten as a dip with slices of red and yellow bell peppers, on Greek dried rusks called *paximathia,* or with breadsticks. This recipe is adapted from one by Diane Kochilas, a Greek food expert with whom I toured Greece.

¼ cup extra-virgin olive oil, preferably Greek

2 cloves garlic, chopped

½ teaspoon red pepper flakes

2 cups crumbled feta cheese (about 1 pound)

3 or 4 bottled pickled red bell peppers, drained and cut into 1-inch pieces

In a small skillet over medium heat, warm the olive oil. Add the garlic and cook until it starts to turn translucent, 1 to 2 minutes. Sprinkle in the pepper flakes and cook for 30 seconds longer. Remove from the heat.

Place the garlic mixture in a food processor and add the feta and drained peppers. Pulse until smooth, stopping to scrape down the sides of the bowl every now and again. Transfer to a bowl, and cover and store in the refrigerator for at least 1 hour before serving. The texture will thicken slightly and the flavors will deepen. Serve as directed in the introduction.

Tapenade
Serves 6 to 8

This pungent sauce from the south of France combines my favorite elements—olives, garlic, anchovies, capers, and, of course, olive oil. Serve it with flat bread, as a spread for *crostini*, or as a dip for raw vegetables (red bell pepper and fennel strips are good). It keeps well in the refrigerator for at least a week; to avoid dryness, pour in a little olive oil to form a film over the top before you store it. Allow to return to room temperature before serving, then mix the extra oil into the sauce.

1 cup pitted Niçoise olives, rinsed and patted dry

2 cloves garlic, minced

2 to 4 oil-packed anchovy fillets, rinsed and patted dry

2 to 3 tablespoons capers, preferably salt-cured, rinsed and patted dry

1 teaspoon fresh lemon juice

Grated zest of ½ lemon

6 tablespoons mild extra-virgin olive oil, preferably French, or as needed

½ teaspoon freshly cracked black pepper

Splash of brandy (optional)

¼ cup chopped fresh Italian parsley (optional)

In a mortar, combine the olives, garlic, anchovies, capers, lemon juice and zest, 6 tablespoons olive oil, pepper, and the brandy, if using. Pound and grind with a pestle. (Alternatively, combine the ingredients in a food processor and pulse briefly.) Add a little more olive oil if the mixure is too thick. The tapenade should be coarse and well textured. Transfer to a small bowl and garnish with the parsley, if you choose.

54

Taramosalata
Makes 2 to 3 cups

Whipped, fluffy *taramosalata* is a favorite Lenten dish in Greece, where it is served with olives, bread or crackers, boiled wild greens, or baked or boiled potatoes. *Tarama*, which is carp or mullet roe, can be found in the refrigerated section of Greek and Middle Eastern specialty stores. Serve this creamy mixture on crackers, toasted pita triangles, or sliced tomatoes.

1 cup water

4 slices white or whole-wheat bread, crusts removed

1/4 pound *tarama*, preferably fresh (see introduction)

2 to 3 tablespoons fresh lemon juice, or to taste

Grated zest of 1 lemon

1/3 cup finely chopped white onion

1/4 cup chopped fresh Italian parsley

3/4 to 1 cup extra-virgin olive oil, preferably Greek

Splash of water

Chopped fresh Italian parsley for garnish (optional)

Put the water in a bowl and slip the bread into it. When fully moistened, squeeze out the moisture and place the bread in a food processor. Add the *tarama*, lemon juice and lemon zest, onion, and 1/4 cup parsley. Pulse to combine. With the motor running, pour in 3/4 cup olive oil in a thin, steady stream, then add the water. Taste and add more olive oil and/or lemon juice as desired. If the mixture tastes too sharp, add more soaked and squeezed bread. Allow to stand for an hour or two before serving.

Serve on a plate or in a shallow bowl. Scatter parsley over the top, if desired.

55

Yellow Pepper Soup
Serves 4 to 6

This bright and colorful soup, known as *passato di peperoni gialli*, was served during the olive harvest at Cibreo, the wonderful Florentine restaurant. It tastes great and looks beautiful with a cross of oil—preferably new green Tuscan oil—drizzled over the top.

5 tablespoons extra-virgin olive oil, preferably Tuscan

1 red onion, finely chopped

1 carrot, peeled and finely chopped

1 celery stalk, finely chopped

4 yellow bell peppers, seeded and coarsely chopped

4 Yellow Finn or russet potatoes, peeled and coarsely chopped

2 bay leaves

1 tablespoon fresh thyme leaves

3 to 4 cups chicken stock, preferably homemade

About 1 cup low-fat or whole milk

1 to 2 teaspoons salt

3 slices white bread, cut into 1-inch cubes

Extra-virgin olive oil for drizzling

In a deep, heavy soup pot over medium heat, warm 2 tablespoons of the olive oil. Add the onion, carrot, and celery and cook, stirring often, until golden brown, 7 to 10 minutes. Add the yellow peppers and potatoes and mix well. Then add the bay leaves, thyme, and chicken stock to cover. If the stock does not quite cover the vegetables, add water to make up the difference. Bring to a boil, reduce the heat to medium-low, and simmer until the potatoes are tender when pierced with a fork, about 30 minutes. Remove from the heat, and remove and discard the bay leaves.

Pass the mixture through a food mill (to remove the skins of the peppers) placed over a clean saucepan. If you do not have a food mill, process the soup in a food processor, in batches, and then pass the purée through a fine sieve, pressing it through with the back of a wooden spoon. Place the pan over medium-low heat. Add enough milk to create a thick but still soupy consistency. Season to taste with salt and reheat.

Meanwhile, warm the remaining 3 tablespoons olive oil in a heavy skillet over medium heat. Add the cubed bread and cook, tossing, until golden brown, 3 to 5 minutes. Using a slotted spoon, transfer to paper towels to drain.

When the soup is hot, ladle it into warmed bowls, sprinkle the croutons on top, and serve at once.

Note: For a sublime consistency and an extra step, Cibreo chef Fabio Picchi suggests that after the soup has been passed through the food mill or sieve, it should be put into a blender, about $1\frac{1}{2}$ cups at a time, and blended for 30 seconds. Then reheat the soup in a clean pan.

Wild Mushroom Soup with Barley and Herbs

Serves 4 to 6

⁂

Mushroom and barley soup is a lovely winter dish that can be a whole meal when served with good dense bread and a salad, such as Arugula and Spinach with Fried Prosciutto, Pine Nuts, and Dried Figs on page 102. This recipe comes from Robert Schneider, who was my first chef at Pier 23 Cafe in San Francisco.

1 pound fresh portobello mushrooms

¼ to ½ pound fresh porcini and/or chanterelle mushrooms

¼ cup mild extra-virgin olive oil

6 shallots, finely chopped

2 cloves garlic, finely chopped

4 large fresh sage leaves, chopped

1 teaspoon each chopped fresh mint, oregano, and thyme

½ teaspoon chopped fresh rosemary leaves

¼ cup chopped fresh Italian parsley

2 cups water

4 cups homemade chicken stock or canned reduced-sodium, reduced-fat chicken broth

¾ cup pearl barley, rinsed

1 pound spinach, carefully rinsed, dried, stemmed, and finely shredded

4 to 6 thin French bread slices (or twice as many if the slices are small), toasted and brushed on one side with extra-virgin olive oil

Grated Parmesan cheese (optional)

Dry sherry (optional)

Olive oil to drizzle into bowls

Brush off any dirt from the mushrooms and then wipe with a damp towel. Trim off the stems and dice the mushroom caps.

In a large soup pot over medium heat, warm ¼ cup olive oil. Add the shallots and garlic and sauté until they become translucent, 1 to 2 minutes. Add the mushrooms and cook, stirring, until they give off a little liquid, then stir in all of the herbs. Once the mushrooms have softened and are well coated with oil, after a few minutes, add the water and stock or broth and bring to a boil. Stir in the barley, reduce the heat to low, and cook until the barley is just tender, about 45 minutes.

Stir in the spinach and cook briefly until wilted. Ladle into warmed bowls and top with the toasted bread slices. If desired, sprinkle with Parmesan and add a small splash of sherry to each bowl. Drizzle with olive oil.

Provençal Garlic Soup

Serves 4

———— ✛ ————

This exceptional yet simple soup looks and tastes creamy, but as a result of the addition of eggs and cheese rather than cream. Simmering the garlic in the stock removes most of its aroma, but none of its flavor. Prepare the soup just before serving, as reheating can curdle the eggs. Serve with a crisp green salad, a fruity extra-virgin olive oil, and extra croutons on the side.

2 heads garlic, separated into cloves and peeled

4 cups homemade chicken stock or canned reduced-sodium, reduced-fat broth

2 teaspoons chopped fresh thyme, or 1 teaspoon dried thyme

4 thin slices French bread

3 to 4 tablespoons fruity extra-virgin olive oil, preferably French

2 eggs

1/3 cup grated Parmesan cheese

Salt and freshly cracked pepper to taste

In a soup pot over medium heat, combine the whole garlic cloves, chicken stock or broth, and thyme. Bring to a boil, reduce the heat to medium, and cook until the garlic can be easily pierced with a fork, about 10 minutes.

Meanwhile, toast the bread slices and brush on one side with some of the olive oil. Set aside.

In a small bowl, combine the eggs and cheese and whisk together with a fork. Whisk a few tablespoons of the hot soup into the egg mixture, then pour the mixture into the soup pot, while stirring constantly. Season with salt and pepper.

Ladle the soup into warmed bowls, top with the toasted bread slices, and drizzle some of the remaining olive oil over each bowl. Serve at once.

59

Pasta, Risotto, & Polenta

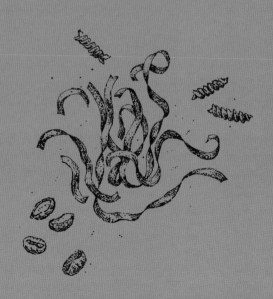

Spaghetti with Garlic, Olive Oil, and Chili

Serves 4

This simple pasta dish, called *spaghetti aglio, olio, e peperoncino*, shows off olive oil like few others do. Put the dish together whenever time is short—it takes only minutes from stove to table. Since the ingredients are uncomplicated, the oil should be very good—use your best.

¾ pound spaghetti

¼ cup extra-virgin olive oil

3 or more cloves garlic, chopped

¼ teaspoon red pepper flakes

Salt and freshly ground pepper to taste

Grated Parmesan or pecorino cheese (optional)

Put a large pot of salted water on a stove and bring to a boil. When the water is boiling, add the pasta and cook until al dente, 8 to 10 minutes.

At the same time, in a medium skillet over medium heat, warm the olive oil. Add the garlic and sauté until translucent, 1 to 2 minutes. Add the pepper flakes.

Drain the pasta and transfer to a warmed serving bowl. Add the contents of the skillet and toss well. Season with salt and pepper and pass the grated cheese at the table, if desired.

Two Pestos

The word *pesto* comes from the Italian verb *pestare,* meaning "to pound." Chef and cookbook author Paul Bertolli speaks forcefully in defense of using a mortar and pestle to make the famed Ligurian sauce: "Handmade pesto has a pleasing coarseness and a lack of uniformity; the blender makes a slick imitation of the original." So, forgo the ease and speed of a food processor or blender, and get the wonderful taste and texture of this traditional basil sauce the way it should be made—by hand.

I have also included a nontraditional pesto recipe, made with fennel greens. The leaves are less delicate than those of the basil plant and the sauce does not suffer from being made in a blender.

Basil Pesto

Makes about 1 cup

This assertive green sauce was a favorite of Genoese sailors who, according to food historian Waverly Root, "found in its basil and garlic the green freshness and the earthy pungency they craved." The sauce can be stirred into a minestrone or used to make *gnocchi alla genovese* (made with potatoes) and *gnocchi verdi* (made with spinach). I love it on pasta or on a hard roll with grilled chicken breast and grilled eggplant. Since it's a Ligurian sauce, an olive oil from that region would be fitting.

$\frac{1}{3}$ cup pine nuts

$2\frac{1}{2}$ cups fresh basil leaves

$\frac{1}{4}$ teaspoon salt

4 cloves garlic

$\frac{1}{2}$ to $\frac{3}{4}$ cup extra-virgin olive oil, preferably Ligurian

$\frac{3}{4}$ cup grated Parmesan cheese, preferably Parmigiano Reggiano

Freshly ground pepper to taste

In a small skillet over medium heat, toast the pine nuts for 1 to 2 minutes to bring out their flavor and to give them a bit of a crunch. Remove from the heat.

Line up the basil leaves spine to spine on a cutting board and cut into julienne. Combine the salt and garlic in a mortar. Using a pestle, mash into a paste. Add the pine nuts and continue to combine with the pestle until the nuts are ground. Add the basil strips a few at a time, incorporating them gradually into the nut mixture. Add a splash of the olive oil, and grind the mixture until it becomes loose. Continuing to grind, add the grated cheese, the pepper, and as much of the remaining olive oil as needed to form a good consistency. The pesto can be transferred to a jar, topped off with a thin film of olive oil, covered tightly, and refrigerated for a few days. But it is never better than the minute you make it, as its color darkens and its flavor changes.

63

Spaghetti with Wild Fennel Pesto Angelo Garro

Serves 6

Angelo Garro is one of the best cooks I know. He's a Sicilian who loves to hunt and gather foods from the wilds of the Bay Area. A few years ago, he introduced me to something that has been growing on my street all my life—wild fennel. The first seeds were carried to California by early Italian immigrants and now the fennel plant grows as a weed in and around San Francisco and Los Angeles.

Harvest wild fennel shoots in winter and spring months when they are young, tender, and bright green. After washing carefully (dogs shy away from fennel because of its strong anise odor), blanch the young shoots in boiling water for a few minutes, drain, and cool. The blanched fennel can be frozen in lock-top bags for later use.

4 to 6 quarts water

1 tablespoon salt

Tender wild fennel greens to yield 4 cups chopped (see introduction)

2 to 3 cloves garlic

$^1\!/_2$ cup grated pecorino cheese

$^1\!/_4$ cup homemade bread crumbs, from day-old bread torn and shredded in a food processor

2 medium eggs

$^1\!/_2$ teaspoon red pepper flakes

Salt and freshly ground black pepper to taste

2 tablespoons extra-virgin olive oil

Splash of dry white wine

$^3\!/_4$ to 1 pound spaghetti, preferably fresh

Extra-virgin olive oil for drizzling

Grated pecorino cheese for sprinkling

In a large pot, bring the water to a boil. Add the salt and the fennel greens and cook for 10 minutes. Drain, reserving the cooking water. Chop the fennel; you will need 4 cups. (Tip: Place the colander over the pot in which you will be cooking the pasta, and drain the fennel into it. Scoop out $1^1\!/_2$ cups of the water to use for the pesto.)

In a food processor, chop the garlic. Add the fennel greens, the $^1\!/_2$ cup pecorino, bread crumbs, eggs, red pepper flakes, and salt and black pepper. Process until puréed.

In a large cast-iron or other heavy skillet over medium heat, warm the 2 tablespoons olive oil. Add the fennel mixture, white wine, and the $1^1\!/_2$ cups reserved fennel cooking water, $^1\!/_2$ cup at a time, adding more water as each addition evaporates. Cook and stir for 5 minutes until the mixture has reduced slightly and the ingredients are well integrated. Remove from the heat and keep warm.

Meanwhile, as the fennel mixture simmers gently, add more water to the fennel water in the pasta pot and bring to a boil. Add the spaghetti and cook until al dente, 1 to 2 minutes for fresh pasta and 8 to 10 minutes for dried. Drain and transfer the pasta to a warmed serving bowl. Add the fennel mixture and toss well. Drizzle with olive oil and sprinkle with pecorino. Serve at once.

Pasta, Risotto, & Polenta

Fettuccine with Asparagus, Fava Beans, and Peas

Serves 4 to 6

This pasta dish, comprised of a trio of bright spring vegetables and a slightly salty grated cheese, is great for serving company because the elements can be prepared ahead of time and then combined at the last minute while the noodles are cooking. If you are using fresh fettuccine, watch the noodles very carefully, as they will be ready in barely 2 minutes. The vegetables can be used in any proportions you like; the amounts that follow are only suggestions.

About $1/2$ pound fresh crab meat would be good with this combination, especially if you use "O" Olive Oil, California Mission olives crushed with Meyer lemons, or an Italian Agrumato, which is also crushed with lemons. If you use crab, don't use cheese. Sprinkle the crab meat on top just before serving, and make sure you season the pasta sufficiently with salt and pepper.

Splash of extra-virgin olive oil, preferably Tuscan

$1 1/2$ cups vegetable stock, reduced over high heat to $3/4$ cup

3 cups asparagus tips, cut on the diagonal into pieces 1 inch long; peeled and shelled fava beans (see note); and young, tender shelled peas, in any combination

$3/4$ pound fettuccine, preferably fresh

Salt and freshly ground pepper to taste

Extra-virgin olive oil, preferably Tuscan, for drizzling

$1/4$ pound pecorino cheese, for both shaving and grating

Put a large pot of salted water on a stove and bring to a boil.

In a large, heavy skillet, over medium heat, warm the splash of olive oil. Add the reduced vegetable stock and simmer for 1 minute. Add the asparagus, favas, and peas and continue to cook over medium heat for 2 minutes.

Meanwhile, add the pasta to the boiling water and cook until al dente, about 2 minutes for fresh noodles and 8 to 10 minutes for dried. Drain, reserving $1/4$ to $1/3$ cup of the pasta water. Add the pasta to the skillet and stir and toss over medium-low heat, adding enough of the pasta water to coat the noodles nicely with the sauce. Transfer to a warmed serving bowl and season with salt and pepper. Drizzle on a little olive oil. Using a vegetable peeler, shave some of the pecorino directly over the top. Pass a bowl of grated pecorino at the table.

Note: One pound of fresh favas in the shell will render about 1 cup of peeled fava beans. Choose firm, bright green pods. Remove the beans as you would peas from a pod. Drop them into a pot of boiling water for 1 minute. Drain and plunge them into ice water to stop the cooking, to keep them bright green, and to aid in the peeling of the skins. After draining again, carefully slip the skin off each fava bean. If the beans are very small and tender, you need not peel them.

Linguine with Gorgonzola Sauce

Serves 4

Landscape architect Nancy Leszczynski loves to work in her garden in the Tuscan hills. When she has friends coming for dinner and has a hard time pulling herself from the garden until sunset, this is what she cooks.

¼ cup extra-virgin olive oil

2 cloves garlic, minced

½ pound Gorgonzola cheese, rind removed, cut into pieces

3 tablespoons pine nuts

¾ pound linguine

3 tablespoons chopped fresh Italian parsley (optional)

Put a large pot of salted water on a stove and bring to a boil.

Bring water in the bottom of a double boiler to a boil.

Meanwhile, in a small skillet over medium heat, warm 1 teaspoon of the olive oil. Add the garlic and sauté until translucent, 1 to 2 minutes. Remove from the heat.

Put the garlic, Gorgonzola, and the remaining olive oil in the top part of the double boiler and place over the lower pan of boiling water. Using a wooden spoon, stir until the mixture almost foams and starts to thicken slightly, about 3 minutes. Turn off the heat under the double boiler.

In a small skillet over medium heat, toast the pine nuts for 1 to 2 minutes to bring out their flavor and give them a bit of a crunch. Remove from heat.

Add the noodles to the boiling water and cook until al dente, 9 to 11 minutes. Drain and transfer to a warmed serving bowl. Add the melted gorgonzola sauce and toss well. Sprinkle with the pine nuts and the parsley, if using. Serve at once.

Spaghetti with Lemony Seared Scallops

Serves 4 to 6

Here is a stylish pasta that requires only minutes to make. I suggest using an inexpensive extra-virgin oil for searing the scallops, then topping the pasta with a very good mild extra-virgin oil, Ligurian perhaps, or an oil that has been crushed with lemons such as the Colona Estate Granverde oil from the Molise in Italy, or "O" Olive Oil from California. This creation was inspired by chef Joe Simone of Boston.

¾ to 1 pound bay scallops or sea scallops

½ cup white flour, preferably Wondra

Salt and freshly ground pepper to taste

2 tablespoons extra-virgin olive oil for searing scallops (see introduction)

Juice of 1 lemon

¾ pound spaghetti

⅓ cup chopped fresh Italian parsley

Grated zest of 1 lemon

2 tablespoons highest-quality mild extra-virgin or lemon-flavored olive oil for drizzling (see introduction)

Put a large pot of salted water on a stove and bring to a boil. Meanwhile, if using bay scallops, leave whole; if using sea scallops, cut into quarters. In a large bowl, combine the flour with the salt and pepper. Dust the scallops with the seasoned flour, then tap off the excess.

Heat a cast-iron skillet over high heat for 1 minute. Add the 2 tablespoons olive oil and warm for 30 seconds. Add the scallops and sear, turning as necessary, for not more than 1 to 2 minutes. Add the lemon juice to the pan and stir. Remove from the heat and cover to keep warm.

Add the pasta to the boiling water and cook until al dente, 8 to 10 minutes. Drain, reserving about ¼ cup of the pasta water. Transfer the pasta to a warmed serving bowl. Add the warm scallops and the pasta water and toss well. Sprinkle the parsley and lemon zest on top, and drizzle with the 2 tablespoons mild extra-virgin olive oil or lemon-flavored oil. Serve at once.

68

Orecchiette with Cauliflower and Pecorino

Serves 4

My childhood friends Cal and Patty Dinner have lived in Italy and are excellent Italian cooks. Each told me about this dish the same week. They love it because it's quick and surprisingly tasty. The cauliflower and the pasta are cooked at the same time in the same pot so they melt into each other.

A few days after I tried this recipe, my godson Christian McIntosh came for lunch and a little cooking lesson. He entered my kitchen and withdrew at the sight of a head of cauliflower on my cutting board—not one of his favorite foods. I begged him to trust me. He did, he loved it, and now this dish is in his repertoire.

³/₄ pound orecchiette or penne

1 head cauliflower, cut into small florets

¹/₄ to ¹/₃ cup extra-virgin olive oil

¹/₃ cup grated pecorino cheese

Chopped fresh Italian parsley

Salt and pepper to taste

Put a large pot of salted water on a stove and bring to a boil. Add the pasta and cauliflower to the boiling water at the same time and cook until the pasta is al dente, 8 to 10 minutes. Drain and transfer to a warmed serving bowl. Add the olive oil and toss well. Sprinkle with the pecorino and parsley, season with salt and pepper to taste, and serve at once.

Variation: To make a crunchy bread crumb topping, remove the crusts from 2 thick slices of day-old bread and tear into small pieces. Place in a food processor and pulse until most of the bread pieces are about the size of small fava beans. You should have about ²/₃ cup. Heat 1¹/₂ tablespoons olive oil in a skillet over medium heat. Stir in the bread crumbs and cook for a few minutes until golden brown. Transfer to a paper towel to crisp. Sprinkle over the pasta along with the grated cheese and parsley.

Linguine with Clams Doused with Basil and Parsley

Serves 4 to 6

Here is tasty pasta that is a Friday night tradition at the Dolphin Club, a swimming and rowing club on San Francisco Bay. The sauce can be made during the time it takes to cook the noodles. Use a mild Ligurian extra-virgin olive oil, if possible; a strong-flavored oil will overpower the flavor of the clams.

⅓ cup mild extra-virgin olive oil, preferably Ligurian

3 or more cloves garlic, thinly sliced

2 to 3 pounds small littleneck clams (24 to 36), scrubbed

Splash of dry white wine

¾ pound linguine

½ cup fresh Italian parsley leaves, roughly chopped

½ cup fresh basil leaves, cut into narrow julienne strips

Pinch of red pepper flakes

Salt and freshly ground black pepper to taste

Extra-virgin olive oil, preferably Ligurian, for drizzling

Lemon wedges

Put a large pot of salted water on a stove and bring to a boil.

Meanwhile, warm the olive oil over medium heat in a skillet large enough to hold all the clams eventually. Add the garlic and sauté until translucent and barely golden, about 2 minutes. Add the clams and wine, cover, and raise the heat to medium-high. Cook until the clam shells pop open, about 7 minutes. Remove from the heat.

Discard any clams that did not open and transfer the remainder to a bowl. Cover with a kitchen towel to keep warm. Strain the cooking juices through a fine-mesh sieve (lined with cheesecloth, if possible) into a small bowl. Remove about two-thirds of the clams from their shells and add them to the strained juices.

While the clams are cooking, add the linguine to the boiling water and cook until al dente, 9 to 11 minutes.

Drain, reserving ¼ cup of the pasta water. Transfer the pasta to a warmed serving bowl. Add the shelled clams and their cooking juices and the pasta water. Toss well. Add the parsley, basil, pepper flakes, and salt and black pepper and again toss well. Scatter the remaining clams in their shells over the top.

Drizzle a little olive oil over the pasta and serve immediately with the lemon wedges on the side.

Green Tagliolini with Chicken Livers, Grappa, and White Truffles

Serves 2 to 4

One rainy night while staying in Greve-in-Chianti, a group of us went to a local restaurant called le Cernacchie, in the neighboring village of La Panca. We were the only customers in the tiny establishment and we each decided to order a different dish and to share. When I took the first bite of my chicken liver pasta, *fili d'abe con grappa e tartufo*, I called the waiter over and asked him to prepare another dish *subito*. I loved my choice and simply could not bear to share it. The combination of the pungent chicken livers, sweet onions, sharp grappa, and aromatic truffle made the dish sublime.

The chef at le Cernacchie used an artisanal bottle of grappa infused with fresh truffles made in nearby San Miniato. Since such an ingredient is hard to come by in the United States, you can do one of two things: Buy a small bottle of grappa and add slices of white truffle. Place the bottle on a sunny windowsill and allow the slices to infuse the grappa for about four days. Or buy any good grappa for flambéing the chicken livers, and then drizzle the finished dish with truffle oil. The latter is probably the easiest, and is the method I have used here.

3 tablespoons fruity extra-virgin olive oil, preferably Tuscan

3 tablespoons unsalted butter

1 large yellow onion, finely chopped

1/2 pound chicken livers, trimmed and cut into 1/2-inch pieces

2 to 3 tablespoons grappa

1/2 pound green tagliolini, preferably fresh

1/3 cup chopped fresh Italian parsley

1 tablespoon or more truffle oil

In a skillet over medium heat, warm the olive oil with the butter. Add the onion, reduce the heat to low, and cook slowly, stirring occasionally, until barely caramelized, about 30 minutes.

Add the chicken livers and cook slowly over medium-low heat until they begin to brown, 10 to 15 minutes. Raise the heat and carefully add the grappa. Ignite the grappa with a match and let the flames die down. Stir to integrate the flavors and keep warm.

Meanwhile, put a large pot of salted water on a stove and bring to a boil. Add the pasta to the boiling water and cook until al dente, about 2 minutes for fresh pasta and 6 to 8 minutes for dried. Drain, reserving 1/4 cup pasta water.

Add the pasta and the pasta water to the skillet. Stir and toss over low heat to combine. Add the parsley, toss well, and transfer to a warmed serving bowl. Anoint the pasta with the truffle oil and serve. This pasta is very rich and is best without grated cheese.

Risotto with Prosciutto and Fresh Peas
Serves 4

Paul Bertolli, chef and part owner of Oliveto Restaurant in Oakland, California, is a risotto master. He calls it "a great simmering stew, where a number of elements surrender their individual identity to the greater purpose of a unified flavor." While he feels what can be included is limitless, "a risotto is best when the number of ingredients is kept to a minimum and each is harmonious with the others."

A risotto is only as good as what goes into it. Carnaroli rice is the Cadillac of Italian rices, producing creamy kernels with a fine texture that absorb liquid well. Superfino Arborio rice is the grade most often used to make risotto, and it's very good, too. In both cases, the shape of the grain—nearly round—is important to ensure the best absorption of the liquid and the ideal showcasing of the flavors of the other ingredients. The rice and liquid merge to form a consistency that northern Italians call *all'onda*, "with waves," where each grain is creamy yet firm.

To make an excellent risotto, an excellent stock that reflects the character of the risotto must be used—seafood stock for a shellfish risotto, chicken stock for subtler flavors, and so on. Here, a light chicken stock marries the salty flavor of the prosciutto with the sweetness of young, tender spring peas. An excellent olive oil, such as a mild, buttery oil from Liguria, would be great. Risottos are often made with butter, but this one works well with olive oil.

4 to 5 cups homemade chicken stock or canned reduced-sodium, reduced-fat broth

2 tablespoons extra-virgin olive oil

1 leek, white part only, well rinsed and finely chopped

1 cup Carnaroli or Arborio rice (see introduction)

1½ ounces thinly sliced prosciutto, diced

¾ cup dry white wine

1 cup young, tender shelled peas

½ cup grated Parmesan cheese, preferably Parmigiano Reggiano

Extra-virgin olive oil for drizzling

Pour the stock or broth into a saucepan and place over medium heat. Bring to a simmer and adjust the heat to keep the liquid at a very gentle simmer throughout the making of the risotto.

In a heavy 4-quart saucepan over medium heat, warm the 2 tablespoons olive oil. Add the leek and sauté until translucent, about 4 minutes. Add the rice and cook, stirring often to prevent the rice from sticking to the bottom and to make sure all grains are coated with hot oil, for 3 minutes.

72

Add the prosciutto and continue to cook until softened, about 2 minutes longer. Then add the wine and cook, stirring, until it is completely absorbed.

Add about $1^1/_2$ cups of the hot stock or broth to cover the rice barely. Stir to combine the ingredients, reduce the heat, and continue to simmer gently, stirring often. As the rice absorbs the liquid, stir in more simmering liquid, $^1/_4$ cup at a time, stirring often. Continue to add the liquid, waiting until each addition is absorbed before adding more. Do not add more liquid than just enough to form a veil over the rice, and add it slowly. Never rush the process. The amount of stock or broth you will need will vary according to how the particular rice absorbs the liquid. Do not worry if you don't need all the liquid.

After about 15 minutes, add the peas. Cook for 5 minutes more, then add the cheese. Taste for texture and seasoning. The rice should be loose and free of clumps and be firm yet creamy. The balance between liquid and grain is vital: too much stock and the rice will separate; too little and the rice will be sticky.

Transfer to a warmed serving dish and drizzle a little extra-virgin olive oil over the top. Spoon into warmed shallow soup bowls to serve.

Wild Mushroom Polenta with Escarole Salad

Serves 4 to 6

I like the coarse-grained polenta available from Gray's Grist Mill in Rhode Island (see Sources, page 162). Of course, any polenta can be used for this recipe, but you will need to shorten the cooking time if you are using a fine-grained cornmeal.

Boston chef Joe Simone inspired this autumn-winter combination. You must soak the mushrooms first, as the polenta will be cooked in the soaking water. The *cavolo nero*, sometimes called black cabbage or Tuscan kale, is a curved, crinkled leaf with some blackish coloring on the green, hence the name. Offer this intriguing dish as a main course or as a side dish to Beef Fillets Sautéed with Balsamic Vinegar (page 98).

Mushrooms:

1 ounce dried porcini mushrooms

2 cups boiling water

Escarole salad:

1 medium head escarole, tough outer leaves discarded

1 bunch Italian black cabbage (*cavolo nero*) or spinach

¼ cup extra-virgin olive oil

3 cloves garlic, minced

12 cherry tomatoes, cut in half (yellow or orange is beautiful, but red is fine)

1 lemon

Salt and freshly ground pepper to taste

Polenta:

4 cups water

2 tablespoons fruity extra-virgin olive oil

1 tablespoon salt

1 cup coarse-grain polenta

1 tablespoon minced fresh sage, or 1½ teaspoons dried sage

Salt and pepper to taste

1 tablespoon unsalted butter or olive oil

¼ to ½ cup grated Parmesan cheese

To prepare the mushrooms, place them in a heatproof bowl, add the boiling water, and let stand for 30 minutes. Scoop out the mushrooms from the water, reserving the water. Place the mushrooms in a sieve, rinse well, and then squeeze out the excess water. Strain the soaking water through a sieve lined with cheesecloth and set aside. Chop the mushrooms roughly and set aside.

To prepare the salad, rinse the escarole and drain well, trim off the tough stem ends, and roughly cut the leaves into 2-inch lengths.

Rinse the cabbage or spinach and drain well, trim off the tough stems, and roughly cut the leaves into 2-inch lengths.

In a large, heavy skillet over medium heat, warm the olive oil. Add the garlic and sauté until translucent, 1 to 2 minutes. Add the escarole and black cabbage or spinach and cook, stirring occasionally, just until they wilt. Add the cherry tomatoes and continue to cook for a few minutes longer. Halve the lemon and squeeze the juice over the top, then season with salt and pepper. Remove from the heat and set aside. (This can be made in advance and reheated just before serving.)

To cook the polenta, in a large heavy saucepan or Dutch oven, bring the water to a boil. Add the olive oil and the salt. With a whisk in one hand and the polenta in a pitcher in the other, pour the polenta into the water in a slow, steady stream, whisking constantly as the water thickens with the polenta. Reduce the heat to medium and, using a wooden spoon, stir continuously for 20 to 30 minutes, adding the reserved mushroom water, a little at a time, when the polenta starts to thicken. (You may need to add a little boiling water if it starts to thicken too quickly.) During the last 10 minutes of cooking, add the mushrooms and sage. The polenta will take on a dark rustic color. It is done when it pulls easily away from the sides of the pot. (At this point, the polenta can be kept warm in a double boiler over simmering water, with the addition of water or stock as needed, for up to an hour.) Remove from the heat.

Stir in the butter or olive oil and $1/4$ cup Parmesan cheese. Taste and adjust the seasoning with salt and pepper. Reheat the escarole salad to serving temperature. Pour the polenta onto a large wooden platter or into a shallow bowl and spoon the escarole mixture into a mound in the center. Serve immediately, passing the remaining Parmesan cheese, if desired.

Fish

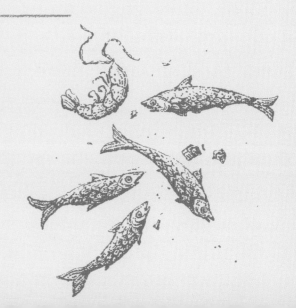

Two Portuguese Fish Stews

Luzia Pinhao is an extraordinary Portuguese cook. She owns a tiny restaurant and takeout on New York's Upper West Side. It's always bustling and filled with lovely aromas. She makes a dense, chewy Portuguese corn bread that is peerless. Even though Luzia comes from Coimbra in northern Portugal, she has lots of fishermen friends from the south, one of whom gave her these recipes. They are her most popular dishes.

Red Snapper in Tomato Broth with Potatoes and Herbs
Serves 4

This stunning, light dish takes only a few minutes to assemble and about 20 minutes to cook. Serve with crusty bread, a bottle of *vinho verde*, and a little extra-virgin olive oil for drizzling on top.

¼ cup extra-virgin olive oil, preferably Portuguese or Spanish

2 medium-sized white potatoes, unpeeled, each sliced into 4 thick rounds

2 yellow onions, each sliced into 5 thick rounds

4 celery stalks, thinly sliced

3 tomatoes, peeled and each cut into 3 thick round slices, or 6 plum tomatoes, peeled and each cut into 2 thick rounds

Salt and freshly ground pepper to taste

1 pound red snapper fillets, cut into 3-inch chunks

1 cup fresh Italian parsley leaves, chopped

2 bay leaves

1 teaspoon dried oregano

½ cup chopped fresh cilantro

1 cup dry white wine

Put the olive oil in a 12-inch flameproof terra-cotta or clay casserole with a lid. Layer the potatoes, onions, celery, and tomatoes on top of the olive oil. Season with a generous sprinkling of salt and pepper. Place over medium heat and bring to a simmer. Cook for a few minutes while you prepare the rest of the ingredients.

Arrange the snapper pieces on top of the vegetables and scatter the parsley, bay leaves, oregano, and cilantro around the fish. Pour in the white wine and, if necessary, add water to cover barely. Cover and continue cooking over medium heat until the fish and vegetables are tender, about 20 minutes. Serve at once.

Pork, Clam, and Chorizo Stew

Serves 2

Here's another quick, delightful stew, with slightly more complicated flavors than the preceding one. The dish is typically served in a *cataplana*, a casserole used for cooking clams, from the Algarve region in the south. Portuguese olive oil tends to be green and a little less intense than Spanish oil, and it can sometimes be slightly minty in flavor. It would be ideal if you could find a bottle for this dish.

6 tablespoons extra-virgin olive oil, preferably Portuguese or Spanish

3 russet potatoes, unpeeled, cut into slices about 2 inches wide by 6 inches long

1 pound chorizo, thinly sliced

6 cloves garlic, chopped

1/2 to 1 pound boneless pork loin, cut into 2-inch-long strips

18 to 24 littleneck clams, scrubbed

1 cup dry white wine

Salt and freshly ground pepper

1 cup fresh Italian leaf parsley leaves, chopped

Preheat an oven to 300 degrees F.

In a large, heavy skillet over medium heat, warm 3 tablespoons of the olive oil. Add the potatoes and fry on all sides until golden brown. Using a slotted spoon or tongs, remove to a wire rack placed over paper towels to drain. Then transfer to an ovenproof platter and place in the oven to keep warm while you complete the dish. Cook the chorizo in the same pan over medium heat, turning as necessary, until lightly browned, 3 to 5 minutes. Using a slotted spoon or tongs, remove to the rack to drain.

Meanwhile, put the remaining 3 tablespoons olive oil in a large flame-proof earthenware dish with a lid or another heavy skillet. Place over medium heat and add the garlic and pork strips. Cook, stirring often, until the pork is no longer pink, 5 to 8 minutes. Add the clams and wine, stir well, and toss in the chorizo. Cover and continue to cook over medium-high heat until all the clam shells pop open, about 7 minutes. Discard any clams that do not open. Season with salt and pepper.

Serve on top of or alongside the fried potatoes. Sprinkle with the chopped parsley. Serve in shallow bowls or individual terra-cotta dishes.

Sea Bass in Parchment

Serves 4 to 6

The delicate white meat steams gently in its parchment package, and when the paper is opened, a fragrant aroma is released. I love to serve this fish with Charmoula I (page 138) on the side. You'll need a roll of cooking parchment 13 to 15 inches wide. Grouper, swordfish, or red snapper can be used in place of the sea bass.

2 pounds sea bass fillet, 1 inch thick and preferably in a single piece

2 tablespoons extra-virgin olive oil

6 thin slices red onion

2 fresh fennel or dill sprigs

6 to 8 lemon slices, each ½ inch thick

1 tablespoon salt-cured capers, rinsed and drained

Freshly cracked pepper to taste

Splash of dry white wine

Salt to taste

Preheat an oven to 400 degrees F.

Cut a piece of parchment twice the size of the piece of fish. Lay the paper on a baking sheet and place the fish in the center (or if you have more than a single piece, place the pieces snugly side by side). Drizzle the fish with the olive oil and arrange the onion slices and the sprigs of fennel or dill on top. Place the lemon slices in a row along the top of the fennel. Scatter the capers on top and sprinkle with the pepper. Splash the assembled fish with a little white wine.

Wrap the paper around the fish and other ingredients and make a tight fold down the length of the fish so no steam will escape. Tuck the ends under the fish. Bake about 30 minutes, possibly longer. To test for doneness, unwrap a corner after 20 minutes and carefully insert a knife; the fish should be opaque at the center. If it is not, rewrap and return to the oven for 10 minutes longer. Watch carefully, as you do not want it to dry out.

Slide the fish bundle onto a warmed serving platter and immediately bring it to the table. Open the bundle, sprinkle the fish with salt, and serve.

North Beach Baccalà with Potatoes, Red Onion, and Parsley

Serves 4 to 6

This salad, based on salt cod (or *baccalà*, in Italian), was first served to me by one of my favorite North Beach cooks, Joe Delgado. The cod's transformation from hard, dried salted fish to a tender-textured salad is magical. Give yourself a day or so from the time of purchase to serving time to allow for soaking the fish. Salt cod is available in most Italian and Greek specialty stores.

In Granada, at a famous restaurant overlooking the Alhambra called El Mirador de Mirayma, I enjoyed an Andalusian salt cod salad similar to this one. To duplicate it, omit the potatoes and add 2 oranges, peeled and sliced, or 4 tangerines, peeled and sectioned; 1/2 cup chopped pitted green olives (6 to 8 olives), and 1 medium tomato, peeled, seeded, and chopped. The orange lends a sweet note to the saltiness of the cod, and it looks pretty with the tomato. This is a variation on a dish called *remojon granadino*.

1 pound skinless, boneless salt cod

1 pound russet potatoes, peeled and cut into eighths lengthwise

2 cups fresh Italian parsley leaves, roughly chopped

1 red onion, thinly sliced

1/2 cup mild extra-virgin olive oil

Freshly ground pepper to taste

Put the salt cod in a large bowl with cold water to cover. Refrigerate for 18 to 24 hours, changing the water at least 4 times.

Drain the salt cod, place in a large saucepan, and add water to cover. Bring to a boil, reduce the heat to medium-low, and simmer until tender when pierced with a knife, 10 to 15 minutes. Do not overcook or it will toughen. Using a slotted spatula or slotted spoon, remove the cod to a large bowl and retain the cooking water. Let the cod cool, then break it up with your fingers, being careful to remove any stray bones or pieces of skin.

Bring the cod cooking water back to a boil and add the potatoes. Cook until tender, 10 to 15 minutes. Drain and add to the bowl of salt cod.

Add the parsley and onion to the fish mixture. Drizzle with the olive oil, add the pepper, and toss gently by hand. Serve at room temperature or refrigerate until serving. The salad will keep refrigerated for up to 3 days, but make sure you bring it to room temperature before serving.

82

FISH

California Crab Cakes on a Bed of Citrus

Serves 6

Crab and fresh lemon are a California tradition. Here, Ralph Tingle, of Bistro Ralph in Healdsburg, California, marries the flavors of Meyer lemon and crab on a sprightly bed of the best of California's citrus crop. If all of the citrus fruits are not available, use as many different kinds as you can find. In the absence of lemon-flavored olive oil, serve with a mild extra-virgin olive oil.

2 lemons, preferably Meyer, and 1 each of the following fruits: medium white grapefruit, medium pink grapefruit, large navel orange, blood orange, lime

1 pound fresh-cooked crab meat, preferably Dungeness, carefully picked over to remove any cartilage or shell fragments

$^{1}/_{2}$ cup Mayonnaise (see page 141) or good-quality store-bought mayonnaise

1 cup freshly made dried bread crumbs

1 egg, lightly beaten

Grated zest of 1 lemon, preferably Meyer

Freshly ground pepper to taste

$^{3}/_{4}$ cup yellow cornmeal

Bulk extra-virgin olive oil for sautéing

Lemon-flavored extra-virgin olive oil/or fruity extra-virgin olive oil for drizzling

1 bunch watercress, tough stems removed

To prepare the citrus, cut a thick slice off the top and bottom of each fruit. Then, working with 1 fruit at a time, stand it upright on a cutting board and, using a sharp knife, cut off the peel in thick strips, removing all the pith and membrane to expose the flesh. Then hold the fruit in the palm of your hand over a bowl and, with the knife, cut along either side of each segment to free it from the membrane, allowing the segments to drop into the bowl. Remove any seeds from the segments with the tip of a knife and arrange the segments on a platter. Drizzle any juice captured in the bowl over the top. Set aside.

In a bowl, combine the crab meat, mayonnaise, $^{1}/_{2}$ cup of the bread crumbs, egg, lemon zest, and pepper. Stir well; the mixture should just hold together without being sticky.

Mix together the remaining $^{1}/_{2}$ cup bread crumbs and the cornmeal in a wide, shallow bowl. Shape the crab mixture into cakes about 2 inches in diameter and $^{3}/_{4}$ inch thick, or smaller if you wish. Gently roll the crab cakes in the cornmeal mixture, coating evenly.

In a large, heavy skillet over medium heat, warm the olive oil for sautéing. Add the crab cakes, in batches, and sauté, turning once, until golden brown and heated through; the timing will depend upon the size of the cakes.

Arrange the hot crab cakes atop the citrus segments and drizzle with lemon-flavored or fruity extra-virgin olive oil. Scatter the watercress sprigs over the platter. Serve at once.

Sea Bass with Capers, Olives, and Pickled Jalapeños

Serves 4

---❧---

The Spanish brought the olive tree to Mexico in the 1700s, where it flourished in the Mediterranean-like climate. Then, so the story goes, Spanish olive growers grew concerned that the New World's oil producers would compete with them, so many of the trees were left untended or were destroyed.

This recipe is adapted from one that appears in a book on Oaxacan food by restaurateur and chef Zarela Martinez. Martinez recommends allowing the finished dish, *pescado en escabeche*, to mellow for 4 hours before eating it, but it tasted so good the first time I cooked it, I served it right away. The use of Spanish olive oil makes this multilayered dish delightful.

5 large fresh parsley sprigs

1 French roll, about 3 ounces, sliced and slices fried on both sides until golden in 2 tablespoons extra-virgin olive oil

6 tablespoons extra-virgin olive oil, preferably Spanish

3 large cloves garlic

1 large white onion, thinly sliced in half-moons

½ teaspoon peppercorns

8 whole cloves

5 bay leaves

1 cup distilled white vinegar

4 sea bass fillets, preferably with skin intact, about 6 ounces each

10 large pimiento-stuffed green olives, sliced into 4 cross-wise pieces

1 tablespoon salt-cured capers, rinsed and drained

2 pickled jalapeño chilies, seeded and thinly sliced

Put the parsley sprigs and bread slices in a food processor and pulse to grind. Set aside.

In a medium sauté pan over medium-high heat, warm 4 tablespoons of the olive oil. Add the garlic and cook, pressing the cloves down with the back of a spoon to release the flavor, until golden, 3 to 4 minutes. Remove and discard the garlic. Add the onion to the pan and sauté until translucent, about 3 minutes. Add the bread-parsley mixture, peppercorns, cloves, and bay leaves and sauté for 5 minutes to blend the flavors. Pour in the vinegar and cook for 1 minute. Remove from heat and let cool.

In a large frying pan over medium-high heat, warm the remaining 2 tablespoons olive oil. Add the fish fillets and fry, turning once, until golden and opaque at the center when cut into with a knife, 2 to 3 minutes on each side. Take care not to overcook them.

Carefully transfer the fish to a serving platter 1 inch deep. Sprinkle the olives, capers, and chilies over the fish and then spoon the cooled vinegar mixture evenly over the top. Let rest for 4 hours (ideally), then serve at room temperature.

86

Seared Ahi Tuna Encrusted with Roasted Pumpkin Seeds

Serves 2 or 3

I first had this at Charles Saunders's East Side Oyster Bar and Grill in Sonoma, California. The pumpkin seeds are rich and crunchy, and the hint of curry mingles nicely with the olive oil and bread crumbs. The flavors and textures stand up to the steaklike quality of the ahi. Other fish fillets can be substituted, such as trout, halibut, or sea bass. Only one side of the fish gets cooked, so pour a little white wine around it to steam it to a perfect finish.

Serve the seed-encrusted tuna on a bed of assorted greens with a basic vinaigrette, or as a main course with Long-Roasted Tomatoes (page 127), Tattooed Potatoes with Rosemary (page 134), and a green salad.

¾ cup pumpkin seeds, coarsely chopped

Salt to taste

¼ cup dried white bread crumbs

¼ cup mild extra-virgin olive oil, preferably French or Ligurian

½ teaspoon paprika

½ teaspoon curry powder

Freshly ground pepper to taste

3 egg whites

1 ahi tuna fillet, about 1 pound and 1 inch thick

Splash of dry white wine

In a heavy skillet over low heat, roast the pumpkin seeds until they begin to pop, then remove from the heat. Sprinkle lightly with salt and pour into a small bowl. Add the bread crumbs, 3 tablespoons of the olive oil, the paprika, curry powder, salt, and pepper. Spread the seed mixture on a flat dish large enough to hold the fish. Place the egg whites in a large bowl and whisk lightly.

Dip the tuna fillet in the egg whites, and then coat well on one side with the pumpkin-seed mixture. In a cast-iron skillet over medium heat, warm the remaining 1 tablespoon olive oil. Add the tuna, seed side up. Cook for 3 minutes, splashing a little white wine around the fish after 2 minutes; do not turn the fish. Remove from the pan and serve.

Grilled Halibut with Chunky Fennel Vinaigrette

Serves 4

Here is a recipe from chef Steve Johnson of the Blue Room in Cambridge, Massachusetts. The chunky fennel vinaigrette also goes well with tuna steaks or swordfish. In fact, Johnson developed this vinaigrette to go with grilled Portuguese sardines. You might try it as a dressing on crisp romaine hearts or ripe tomato slices, or toss it with pasta and sprinkle a little pecorino over the top.

The fish can also be cooked on a stove-top grill or in a cast-iron skillet, adding a little extra-virgin olive oil in both cases.

1 cup chopped fennel

2 shallots, thinly sliced

2 cloves garlic, minced

2 oil-packed anchovy fillets, chopped

1 teaspoon salt-cured capers, rinsed, drained, and minced

1 teaspoon whole-grain mustard

½ teaspoon chopped fresh thyme, or a little less if dried

¼ teaspoon red pepper flakes

¼ cup fresh lemon juice

½ cup fruity extra-virgin olive oil

Salt and freshly cracked black pepper to taste

4 halibut fillets or steaks, each about 1 inch thick and about 1½ pounds total weight

Prepare a fire in a charcoal grill.

Put the chopped fennel, shallots, garlic, anchovies, and capers in a bowl; toss well. Add the mustard, thyme, pepper flakes, lemon juice, and olive oil and stir to mix. Season with salt and pepper.

Place the fish on an oiled grill rack 6 to 8 inches above the fire. Cook for 4 to 5 minutes on each side, turning once. To test for doneness, pierce a piece of fish with a knife; it should be opaque in the center.

Transfer the fish to a warmed platter or individual plates and spoon some of the fennel vinaigrette over the top. Serve the remaining vinaigrette in a bowl alongside.

Grilled Snapper in Grape Leaves with Caper-Lemon Sauce

Serves 4

These Greek-inspired grape-leaf bundles taste best when grilled over charcoal. A branch of rosemary thrown on the coals will give the smoke an appealing woodsy scent. Fresh sardines, sea bass fillets, or any firm fish fillets can be substituted for the snapper. Grape leaves from Middle Eastern specialty stores are sold in jars in brine and must be rinsed before using. If you are using fresh grape leaves, remove the tough stems and blanch the leaves in boiling water for 3 to 5 minutes.

In the winter, these packets can be cooked on a stove-top grill or in a cast-iron skillet, but you'll miss the flavor of the coals.

28 to 32 grape leaves
(see introduction)

1 pound red snapper fillets

Extra-virgin olive oil, preferably Greek, for brushing

Shredded zest of 2 lemons

14 to 16 fresh dill sprigs or
fennel sprigs

Salt and freshly ground pepper
to taste

Caper-lemon sauce:

$\frac{1}{3}$ cup extra-virgin olive oil,
preferably Greek

Juice of 1 lemon

1 tablespoon salt-cured capers,
rinsed, drained, and chopped

1 tablespoon finely chopped
fresh dill or fennel tops

Salt and freshly ground pepper
to taste

Prepare a fire in a charcoal grill.

Remove the grape leaves from the brine and rinse in cool water. Dry on kitchen towels.

Cut the fish into 2-inch squares about $\frac{1}{2}$ inch thick, and remove any errant bones. On a platter, overlap 2 grape leaves, stem side up. Place a piece of fish in the center, brush the fish with olive oil, scatter on a little lemon zest, and top with a dill or fennel sprig. Season with salt and pepper. Roll up the fish in the leaves, using a little extra olive oil to seal the bundle. If you feel the bundles might come apart, tie with kitchen string. Brush the outsides with a little olive oil.

To make the sauce, in a small bowl, stir together all the ingredients with a fork.

Place the fish bundles on the grill rack, 6 to 8 inches above the hot coals. Cook for about 4 minutes on each side, turning once with a spatula. To test for doneness, open a bundle and test the fish with a fork; it should be opaque in the center. Arrange the bundles on a warmed platter and pour a little of the sauce over the top. Serve the remaining sauce in a bowl on the side. The grape leaves will be soft and once unfolded, can be eaten with the fish. Alternatively, serve the bundles at room temperature.

Meats

Roasted Chicken with Preserved Lemons and Cracked Green Olives

Serves 4

This is my very simple takeoff on Marcella Hazan's Roast Chicken with Lemons and Paula Wolfert's Moroccan Chicken with (Preserved) Lemons and Olives. Preserved lemons are an indispensable ingredient in Moroccan cooking, used in festive vegetable and lamb stews (*tagines*), stuffed into baked fish, or added to a variety of salads. Make a batch of the lemons (more than you'll need for this recipe) and have them on hand whenever you want a taste of the Maghreb in your food.

Some olives, such as the French Picholine, need to be blanched to remove the sharpness of their brine. Others, such as the Greek Royale, can be so bitter that you need to boil them more than once to eliminate the strong taste before you discover the underlying flavor. So taste your olives first, then decide how to treat them before you add them to a dish.

Preserved lemons:

8 large lemons

1 cup coarse sea salt

1½ to 2 cups fresh lemon juice

Olive oil

1 preserved lemon (8 wedges)

1 chicken, 3 to 4 pounds

3 tablespoons extra-virgin olive oil

¾ cup imported green olives (see introduction)

Freshly cracked pepper

Wash and dry the lemons. Cut each one into eighths lengthwise. Place in a large bowl, add the salt, and toss together. Transfer the lemons to a 2- to 2½-quart jar with a spring top. Pour in the lemon juice to cover. Cover and allow the lemons to remain in a cool, dark spot for 1 week, agitating the jar every couple of days to distribute the salt throughout. Float a little olive oil on top of the lemons, then store in the refrigerator for up to 6 months.

• • • • •

Preheat an oven to 400 degrees F. Rinse the salt off the preserved lemon wedges, and scrape off and discard the pulp. Rinse the chicken inside and out and pat dry. Rub with the olive oil, then stick the preserved lemon rind in the cavity. Place the bird in a roasting pan, breast side up. Roast for 45 minutes to 1 hour without basting.

Meanwhile, pit the olives: Place them between two kitchen towels and run a rolling pin over them a few times, or wack each olive with the flat side of a large kitchen knife. This will help to ease the pits out; you may need to use a small sharp knife to complete the job. Bring a small pan of water to a boil and drop the olives in for a few minutes to remove the bitterness, then drain, rinse, and taste. Repeat if the olives are too bitter. Set aside.

Check the chicken after 45 minutes; if a leg wiggles easily (or if the juices run clear when a thigh is pierced), it is done. Remove from the oven and remove the lemon rind from the cavity. Thinly slice the lemon rind, being careful not to burn your fingers. Scatter the rinds and the olives in the pan juices around the chicken.

Transfer the chicken to a serving platter and carve it. Spoon the olives, sliced lemon rind, and a few tablespoons of the pan juices over the slices. Serve at once.

Butterflied Leg of Lamb Stuffed with Minty Gremolata
Serves 8 to 10

This is a wonderful party dish because it can be cooking while you are having drinks and then served hot with the pan juices, or it can be roasted ahead of time, sliced, and served at room temperature. For a dinner party, accompany it with Baked Tuscan White Beans (page 126) or a double recipe of Caramelized Roasted Vegetables (page 122).

Gremolata stuffing:

2 cups chopped fresh Italian parsley

1/2 cup chopped fresh mint

8 cloves garlic, chopped

Grated zest of 2 lemons

1/2 cup extra-virgin olive oil

Salt and freshly ground pepper to taste

1 boneless leg of lamb, about 5 pounds

2 bay leaves

Bulk extra-virgin olive oil for rubbing on lamb

1/2 cup dry white wine

Salt and freshly ground pepper to taste

Preheat an oven to 400 degrees F.

To make the stuffing, in a bowl, combine all the ingredients and mix well.

Lay the boned leg of lamb flat. Spread the stuffing evenly over the meat and top with the bay leaves. Roll up the lamb into its original shape as best as you can, tie securely with kitchen string, and place in a roasting pan. (Or take the stuffing to your butcher and ask him to stuff, roll, and tie the lamb.) Rub the lamb with olive oil.

Roast the lamb for 15 minutes. Turn and roast for another 15 minutes. Reduce the temperature to 350 degrees F and turn the lamb once more. Continue to cook until done to your liking, 50 to 60 minutes longer for medium-rare (about 1 1/2 hours in all). The flesh should have a springy texture when pressed with your finger, or should register 140 degrees F on a meat thermometer for rare and 145 degrees F for medium-rare. Transfer the lamb to a warmed platter.

Skim off as much fat from the pan juices as possible and place the roasting pan on the stove top over medium-low heat. Bring the juices to a simmer, add the wine, and scrape up any drippings from the pan bottom. Season with salt and pepper. Thinly slice the roast and arrange on the platter. Serve with some of the juices poured over the slices and serve the rest in a gravy boat alongside.

Roasted Chicken with Potatoes, Capers, and Endive

Serves 4

❧

I first had this dish at landscape architect and artist Barbara Stauffacher Solomon's house overlooking San Francisco Bay. We sat on her deck lined with big Italian terra-cotta pots filled with lavender while the dinner cooked all by itself in the kitchen downstairs. When the meal was served, the aroma of the chicken, the olive oil, and other Mediterranean ingredients mingled with the scent of the flowers, making us feel as if we were having dinner on the French Riviera. It's the perfect dish for company because once it goes in the oven, it needs little attention.

1 chicken, 3 to 3 1/2 pounds

3 tablespoons extra-virgin olive oil

1/2 cup fresh lemon juice

Salt and freshly ground pepper to taste

8 or more cloves garlic

6 Belgian endives, ends trimmed and halved lengthwise

1 pound small red potatoes, unpeeled, scrubbed

1 large fresh rosemary sprig

3 tablespoons salt-cured capers, rinsed and drained

Preheat an oven to 450 degrees F. Rinse the chicken inside and out, pat dry, and place in a large roasting pan. Rub the chicken with the olive oil and drizzle with the lemon juice. Season with salt and pepper. Scatter the garlic, endive, and potatoes around the bird. Put the rosemary sprig in the cavity.

Roast for 45 minutes. Scatter the capers around the chicken in the pan juices and continue to roast until a leg wiggles easily (or juices run clear when a thigh is pierced), about 15 minutes longer.

Transfer the chicken to a warmed serving platter. Using a slotted spoon, remove the vegetables from the pan and arrange around the chicken. Skim off and discard the fat from the pan juices. Pour the remaining juices, along with the capers, over the chicken. Carve and serve.

MEATS

OLIVE OIL · FROM TREE TO TABLE

Roasted Chicken Breasts Stuffed with Salsa Verde

Serves 4 to 6

To dress up the ubiquitous chicken breast, stuff this piquant *salsa verde* under the skin and roast as usual. The green sauce, veiled beneath the skin, looks alluring and spices up the meat. The breasts are also wonderful grilled over a medium-hot charcoal grill.

Salsa verde:

3 tablespoons salt-cured capers, rinsed and drained

2 oil-packed anchovy fillets, rinsed and chopped

3 or more cloves garlic, chopped

1 tablespoon fresh lemon juice

Grated zest of 2 lemons

⅓ cup extra-virgin olive oil

2½ cups fresh Italian parsley leaves

6 boneless chicken breast halves, with skin intact

Extra-virgin olive oil for brushing

Preheat an oven to 400 degrees F.

To make the *salsa verde*, in a food processor, combine the capers, anchovy fillets, garlic, lemon juice, and three-fourths of the zest. Purée until smooth. Add the ⅓ cup olive oil and process again until smooth, scraping down the sides of the bowl as necessary. Add the parsley and pulse until combined.

To stuff each chicken breast, gently pull the skin from the meat and tuck one-sixth of the *salsa verde* in the pocket that forms between them, distributing the salsa evenly. Arrange the stuffed chicken breasts in a baking dish and brush them with a little olive oil.

Roast until the chicken breasts are tender, about 30 minutes. Remove from the oven and place on individual plates or a platter. Scatter the remaining lemon zest over the top and serve.

Beef Fillets Sautéed with Balsamic Vinegar

Serves 4

I had this dish at Paparazzi, Joe Simone's restaurant in Boston, and immediately asked for the recipe. Its flavors are so rich and complex that I was surprised at how simple it is to make. Serve with Mashed Potatoes with Celery Root and Horseradish (page 133).

2 tablespoons extra-virgin olive oil

4 filet mignons, each 1 1/2 inches thick, trimmed of all fat

2 tablespoons dry red wine

3 tablespoons beef stock

2 tablespoons balsamic vinegar

1 fresh porcini mushroom, about 2 ounces, sliced 1/2 inch thick (optional)

1 carrot, peeled and cut into 1/4-inch dice

1/2 red onion, cut into 1/4-inch dice

Salt and freshly ground pepper to taste

Place a large, heavy skillet (cast iron is good) over medium-high heat for 2 minutes. Add the olive oil and heat for 30 seconds. Put the meat in the skillet and sear on both sides, turning once and allowing a minute or so on each side. Add the wine, beef stock, and balsamic vinegar. Toss in the mushroom, if using, the carrot, and the onion around the meat. Cook until done to your preference, a few more minutes on each side for rare. Season with salt and pepper. Serve at once with the vegetables piled on top, if you like.

Tenderloin of Pork with Blood Oranges and Dark Rum

Serves 2 to 4

Whenever I prepare this recipe, I am reminded fondly of one of my favorite drinks, Myers' rum and orange juice. Just add meat.

2 blood oranges or Valencia oranges

3 large cloves garlic

1 teaspoon chopped fresh rosemary, or ½ teaspoon dried rosemary

2 tablespoons dark rum

1 tablespoon dark brown sugar

1 tablespoon Worcestershire sauce

2 tablespoons extra-virgin olive oil

1 pork tenderloin, about ¾ pound

Salt and freshly ground pepper to taste

Grate the zest from the oranges, then squeeze out the juice. You should have ½ cup juice. Set aside 1 tablespoon of the zest. Place the remaining zest, all of the juice, the garlic, rosemary, rum, brown sugar, Worcestershire sauce, and 1 tablespoon of the olive oil in a large bowl. Stir well. Add the pork, turn to coat evenly, cover, and let stand for 30 minutes at room temperature or up to 2 hours in the refrigerator.

Preheat an oven to 400 degrees F. In a heavy ovenproof skillet, heat the remaining 1 tablespoon olive oil over high heat. Remove the tenderloin from the marinade, scraping off most of the juice mixture; reserve the juice mixture for later use. Add the tenderloin to the skillet and brown well on all sides. Pour the reserved juice mixture over the browned meat and transfer to the oven. Roast for 12 minutes. Turn over the pork and continue to roast for 5 to 10 minutes longer. Cut into the meat; it should be barely pink. Cook a few minutes longer if you prefer it well done.

Slice the pork into thin pieces and arrange on a warmed platter. Season with salt and pepper. Scatter the remaining orange zest over the sliced meat. Spoon some of the pan juices over the meat and serve the rest in a bowl alongside.

99

Salads

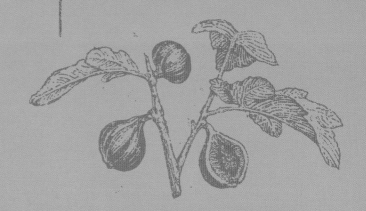

Arugula and Spinach with Fried Prosciutto, Pine Nuts, and Dried Figs

Serves 4

The fried prosciutto gives this salad a mysterious salty quality that is gently balanced by slivers of dried fig.

Dressing:

1 tablespoon fresh lemon juice

1 tablespoon balsamic vinegar

1 teaspoon Dijon mustard

¼ cup fruity extra-virgin olive oil, preferably Tuscan

Freshly ground pepper to taste

Salad:

2 tablespoons bulk extra-virgin olive oil

8 thin slices prosciutto, all fat removed, sliced into long narrow strips

5 tablespoons pine nuts

1 pound baby spinach, carefully rinsed and well dried

2 cups arugula leaves, carefully rinsed and well dried

4 dried figs, very thinly sliced

To make the dressing, in a large salad bowl, whisk together the lemon juice, vinegar, and mustard. Whisk in the olive oil (you may want to add a little more oil, depending upon the strength of the vinegar). Season with pepper.

To make the salad, in a skillet over medium heat, warm 2 tablespoons of olive oil. Add the prosciutto and cook for a few minutes. The slices will turn gray and then red. When they are red, using a slotted spoon, transfer to paper towels to drain.

In a small skillet over medium heat, toast the pine nuts, stirring constantly, for 1 or 2 minutes to bring out their flavor and give them a bit of a crunch. Remove from the heat.

Add the spinach and arugula to the salad bowl and toss with the dressing. Scatter the figs, prosciutto, and pine nuts over the top and serve immediately.

Caesar Salad

Serves 4 to 6

This is one of my favorite recipes. It's strong, aggressive, and very popular, and can make a head of romaine into a meal. I often bring the makings for a Caesar salad when I'm asked to contribute food for a party or when I go away for the weekend. I store the dressing in a jar, and bring along a paper bag filled with homemade croutons and a wedge of Parmesan for grating on top. The dressing can be made with or without the egg. Be sure to refrigerate it if you add the egg. The dressing makes a wonderful dip for raw vegetables or cooked asparagus spears as well.

Dressing:

1 tin (2 ounces) oil-packed anchovy fillets, rinsed and drained

3 to 6 cloves garlic, coarsely chopped

1 egg (optional; see Note)

2 tablespoons fresh lemon juice

1 teaspoon Dijon mustard

¾ cup mild extra-virgin olive oil

¼ cup grated Parmesan cheese, preferably Parmigiano Reggiano

Freshly cracked pepper to taste

Salad:

1 to 2 heads romaine lettuce

¼ cup bulk extra-virgin olive oil

½ baguette, very thinly sliced

About 2 ounces Parmesan cheese, preferably Parmigiano Reggiano

Freshly cracked pepper to taste

To make the dressing, in a food processor, combine the anchovies and garlic and process to mix. Add the egg, if using, most of the lemon juice, and the mustard and process to combine. With the motor running, slowly pour in the olive oil in a thin, steady stream. Add the Parmesan, season with pepper, and process again. Taste, and add as much of the remaining lemon juice as needed to achieve a good balance.

Discard any bruised outer leaves from the romaine heads, then rinse and dry well. In a large, heavy skillet over medium heat, warm the olive oil. Add the baguette slices and cook, turning once, just until they turn golden, a few minutes. Using tongs or a slotted spoon, remove the croutons to a wire rack to drain.

Tear the lettuce leaves into pieces and place in a large salad bowl. Drizzle the dressing over the leaves and toss with your hands until all the leaves are coated. Toss in the croutons. Using a vegetable peeler, shave the Parmesan over the top. Sprinkle with pepper and serve.

Note: Raw eggs have been known to carry salmonella.

Spicy Tunisian Carrot Salad with Caraway, Olives, and Feta

Serves 4 to 6

The spicy-hot bite in this salad, called *houriya*, comes from *harissa*, a savory Tunisian paste made from dried red chili peppers, garlic, olive oil, and salt (see Sources, page 162). Although it would be good to use a Tunisian olive oil for the salad, they are seldom exported to the United States. Most Tunisian oil goes to France and is bottled there as French olive oil.

8 carrots, peeled and sliced into 1/2-inch-thick slices

4 cloves garlic, chopped

1/2 teaspoon salt

2 teaspoons caraway seeds

1 tablespoon *harissa* (see introduction)

6 to 8 tablespoons cider vinegar

1/4 cup extra-virgin olive oil

1 cup crumbled feta cheese

15 to 20 imported black olives such as Kalamata

Bring a saucepan filled with water to a boil. Add the carrots and cook until tender, about 5 minutes. Drain and cool under running cold water, then drain again. Place in a bowl.

In a mortar, combine the garlic, salt, and caraway seeds and grind well until a rough paste forms. Alternatively, pulse the ingredients in a food processor. Add the *harissa* and vinegar and mix well.

Mash the carrots with a fork. Add the garlic-caraway mixture and mix well, then integrate the olive oil. Add most of the cheese and olives and toss again. Transfer to a shallow dish and top with the remaining crumbled feta and olives.

Classic Greek Salad

Serves 6 to 8

This is one of my favorite salads during late summer and early fall when tomatoes are in season. It is an enormously appealing meal on a hot summer day. I like to use yellow, orange, and red tomatoes, and sometimes even tiger-striped green tomatoes. You can make it with cherry tomatoes, too, cutting them in half. Greeks do not usually peel the tomatoes, but you can if you like. Typically, this salad is dressed with olive oil only—no lemon or vinegar. The brine from the olives provides enough pungency and acidity. Use a good fruity Greek olive oil, if you can.

6 large, ripe tomatoes (about 3 pounds), cut into bite-sized wedges (see introduction)

2 cucumbers, peeled, halved lengthwise, seeded, and cut into 1-inch-thick slices

1 large red bell pepper, seeded, cut lengthwise into narrow strips, and each strip cut in half crosswise

1/4 pound Kalamata olives (about 20), pitted

1/2 large red onion, very thinly sliced

1/2 pound feta cheese, crumbled

1/3 cup extra-virgin olive oil, preferably Greek

1 tablespoon dried oregano, preferably Greek

Freshly cracked black pepper to taste

1/4 cup chopped fresh Italian parsley (optional)

In a large salad bowl, combine the tomatoes, cucumbers, red pepper, olives, most of the sliced onion, and most of the feta. Drizzle with the olive oil, and sprinkle with the oregano and cracked pepper. Toss gently. Scatter the remaining feta and onion over the top. Grind a little more pepper over the top, then sprinkle on the parsley, if using. Do not make this salad too far in advance as it gets watery. If that should happen, drain off the excess liquid and add a little more oil.

Mussel Salad with Purple Potatoes

Serves 6 to 8

Small purple potatoes may take a lot longer to grow than other potatoes, and they may not keep as long, but they certainly do look spectacular in this salad next to the blue-black shells of the mussels. Red new potatoes also look and taste good with this slightly French, but decidedly Californian, salad.

12 small new or purple potatoes, unpeeled

¼ cup extra-virgin olive oil

3 cloves garlic, chopped

1 cup dry white wine

2 pounds mussels, scrubbed and debearded

1 tablespoon herbes de Provence, or ½ teaspoon each dried thyme, savory, basil, and marjoram

¼ cup chopped fresh Italian parsley or chervil

3 tablespoons chopped fresh chives

Dash of red pepper flakes

Salt and freshly ground pepper to taste

Place the potatoes in a saucepan with water to cover. Bring to a boil and boil until tender, about 15 minutes. Drain, cut in half, and keep warm.

In a large, heavy skillet over medium heat, warm 1 tablespoon of the olive oil. Add the garlic and sauté for about 2 minutes. Add the wine and bring to a rolling simmer. Add the mussels and herbes de Provence. Cover and cook just until the mussels open, about 5 minutes. Using a slotted spoon, transfer the mussels to a bowl. Discard any mussels that did not open.

Line a fine-mesh sieve with cheesecloth and strain the pan juices through it into a small bowl. Return the juices to the pan and place over medium-low heat. Simmer to reduce the juices by one-half. Remove from the heat and whisk in the remaining 3 tablespoons oil.

If desired, remove all but 6 mussels from their shells; reserve the unshelled mussels for decorating the dish. In a salad bowl, toss the potatoes and mussels with the pan juices. Sprinkle with the parsley or chervil, chives, and pepper flakes. Season with salt and pepper. Arrange the reserved mussels on top. Serve warm.

SALADS

Endive, Watercress, and Shrimp Salad with Port and Stilton Dressing

Serves 4 to 6

This salad was inspired by a visit to the Isle of Man one Christmas season. Every meal was followed by the passing of a huge wheel of Stilton and a bottle of port. Very few vegetables, except Belgian endive and watercress, were available. Prawns and tiny scallops, the latter called Queenies, were easy to come by. When it was my turn to cook a meal, this was what I made; the salad was an enormous hit.

Dressing:

2 large shallots, minced

2 teaspoons Dijon mustard

2 dashes of Worcestershire sauce

1 1/2 tablespoons tawny port

2 teaspoons fresh orange juice

1 teaspoon balsamic or white wine vinegar

3 tablespoons extra-virgin olive oil

Salt and freshly ground pepper to taste

Salad:

3 Belgian endives

1 large bunch watercress, tough stems removed, carefully rinsed, and dried (about 8 cups)

1 to 1 1/2 pounds medium shrimp (30 to 50), peeled and deveined

1/3 cup crumbled Stilton cheese or other blue cheese

1 tablespoon grated orange zest

Prepare a fire in a charcoal grill and oil the rack.

To make the dressing, in a bowl, whisk together all the ingredients. Set aside.

To make the salad, reserve about 8 outer leaves from the endives and cut the remaining leaves into julienne strips. In separate bowls, place the endive and watercress, cover, and chill until after the shrimp are cooked.

When the fire is ready, place the shrimp on the grill rack set about 6 inches above the fire. Grill, turning once, until just cooked through and turning pink, about 1 minute on each side. (The shrimp can instead be cooked on a preheated stove-top griddle or in a cast-iron skillet.)

Toss the julienned endive and the watercress sprigs separately with the dressing and arrange decoratively on a platter with the whole reserved endive leaves and the shrimp. Sprinkle the salad with the cheese and orange zest and serve.

French Lentil Salad
Serves 4 to 6

Lentils have long been eaten in the Middle East and in France. One winter I spent a New Year's with friends in Ramatuelle, a tiny village near St. Tropez. We'd go to the open-air markets to gather our supplies so that we could cook at home. We fell in love with the mild local olive oil and the slate-colored *lentilles du Puy* or *lentilles vertes*, as they are called there, and often combined them in this salad. If you cannot find the *lentilles du Puy* from central France or the *lenticchie* from southern Italy, buy the more common gray-brown variety.

Should you wish to serve these lentils as an accompaniment to meats, serve them hot and omit the lettuce or greens. Otherwise, offer them as a salad over bitter greens at room temperature. The flavor of the salad will intensify as it cools.

2 cups small French lentils (see introduction), picked over, rinsed, soaked in water to cover for 1 hour, and drained

7 cups cold water

1½ teaspoons salt

1 bay leaf

Dressing:

4 cloves garlic, chopped

Shredded zest of 1 lemon

1 teaspoon salt

1 tablespoon Dijon mustard

¼ cup balsamic vinegar

½ cup chopped red onion

½ to ¾ cup mild extra-virgin olive oil, preferably French

Freshly cracked pepper to taste

1 cup fresh Italian parsley leaves, chopped

4 cups bitter greens such as dandelion, frisée, or arugula, or 4 to 6 butter lettuce leaves

Combine the drained lentils, water, salt, and bay leaf in a 3-quart saucepan. Bring to a simmer, skimming off any foam as it appears. Cook just below a rolling simmer for 12 to 15 minutes. The lentils should be tender and still hold their shape. Drain well and remove and discard the bay leaf.

To make the dressing, in a salad bowl, combine the garlic, lemon zest, salt, mustard, vinegar, onion, olive oil, and pepper, whisking well.

Add the drained lentils to the bowl with the dressing and the parsley and toss to mix well. Set aside for 1 hour before serving. Serve on a bed of bitter greens or on individual plates atop butter lettuce leaves.

Fava Bean and Pecorino Salad

Serves 4 to 6

Pythagoras, the sixth-century-B.C. Greek philosopher, warned his followers to avoid fava beans because they make for a noisy stomach and, more significantly, they contain the souls of the dead. Contemporary studies show that fava beans are actually lower in indigestible sugars than most other beans, although strangely enough, many people of the Mediterranean are allergic to them.

Throughout the spring in the Mediterranean, fresh favas are used widely—in salads, in combination with other vegetables, and in pastas and risottos. They are drizzled with olive oil and served alongside a round of goat cheese, and sometimes, after the main course, young, tender favas are passed, still in their pods, so that each guest shells his or her own portion as if they were nuts. In Apulia, dried favas are cooked and puréed with green chicory and swirled with olive oil.

This is indisputably one of the prettiest spring dishes. It can also be made with a crumbly ricotta, as I first had it in Apulia. According to Apulia expert Nancy Harmon Jenkins, "Puliese cooks use garlic sparingly, and the deeper into Pulia you travel, the more likely you will find onions favored over garlic for their sweeter flavor." But I love the flavor of garlic with favas, so I have included it here.

2 pounds fava beans

2 cloves garlic, minced

1 tablespoon chopped fresh mint

1 tablespoon balsamic vinegar

6 to 8 tablespoons extra-virgin olive oil

Salt and freshly ground pepper to taste

1/4 pound pecorino cheese

To shell the fava beans, remove the beans as you would peas from a pod. Bring a saucepan filled with water to a boil, add the favas and blanch for 1 minute. Drain and immerse the favas in ice water to retain their bright green color. Drain again and slip the skin off each fava bean. If the beans are very small and tender, you need not peel them.

In a salad bowl, combine the garlic, mint, vinegar, olive oil, and salt and pepper. Add the favas to the oil mixture. Toss gently. Using a vegetable peeler, shave the pecorino cheese over the top and serve.

Quick White Beans in Olive Oil

Serves 4 to 6

This is a perfect salad to prepare if friends drop by unexpectedly, or if you come home hungry and tired and want to eat something soothing, wonderful, and quick. Serve the beans on slices of toast as a *bruschetta*.

3 cans (14 ounces each) imported white beans, preferably Berni brand, drained, or 3 cups cooked and drained *cannellini* beans

1 large red bell pepper, seeded and diced

1 or 2 ripe tomatoes

6 tablespoons extra-virgin olive oil, preferably Tuscan

2 cloves garlic, chopped

$\frac{1}{4}$ cup chopped red onion

Splash of red wine vinegar

$\frac{1}{2}$ cup chopped fresh Italian parsley

Salt and freshly ground pepper to taste

In a bowl, combine all the ingredients and toss gently. Eat immediately or set aside to marinate for 1 hour before serving.

Variations: Substitute $\frac{1}{2}$ cup julienned fresh basil or arugula leaves for the Italian parsley.

Celery Root Rémoulade

Serves 2 to 4

When I was a student in Paris, this was the one vegetable that I ordered nearly every time I went out for dinner. It was often served as an hors d'oeuvre, as part of an *assiette des crudités* with beet and carrot salads. It was the first dish I made for my family when I returned home.

Juice of 1 lemon

Pinch of salt

1 celery root, about 1 pound

Dressing:

3 tablespoons balsamic vinegar

2 to 3 tablespoons Dijon mustard

2 tablespoons warm water

$\frac{1}{3}$ to $\frac{1}{2}$ cup extra-virgin olive oil

2 to 3 tablespoons mayonnaise (optional)

Salt and freshly ground pepper to taste

$\frac{1}{2}$ cup roughly chopped fresh Italian parsley

Fill a medium-sized bowl with water and add the lemon juice and salt. Bring a saucepan filled with water to a boil. Meanwhile, peel the celery root and cut into julienne strips, grate on the large holes of a grater, or shred in a food processor fitted with the shredding disk. Add the celery root to the boiling water and boil for 2 minutes. Drain and add to the lemon water.

To make the dressing, in a bowl, whisk together the vinegar, mustard, and warm water. Slowly whisk in the olive oil until the dressing becomes creamy. Add the mayonnaise to soften the flavor, if you like.

Drain the celery root and pat dry. Add to the dressing, along with the salt, pepper, and parsley. Toss to coat the celery root evenly and serve.

White Winter Salad of Endive, Fennel, and Shaved Parmesan

Serves 6

I first had this salad at the New York restaurant Barocco, where shaved fennel, arugula, and Parmesan were drizzled with a very good olive oil. When I returned home to San Francisco to a restaurant I then owned, I couldn't wait to add a Belgian endive variation on the New York salad to the menu. A green, fruity olive oil looks and tastes perfect on the white vegetables.

Dressing:

⅓ cup extra-virgin olive oil, preferably Tuscan

3 tablespoons fresh lemon juice

1 clove garlic, minced

Salt and freshly ground pepper to taste

Salad:

3 fennel bulbs

4 Belgian endives

¼ pound Parmigiano Reggiano cheese

½ white onion, very thinly sliced

Green peppercorns to taste

To make the dressing, in a small bowl, whisk together all the dressing ingredients.

To make the salad, trim off the feathery tops and stalks from the fennel bulbs. Cut off any bruised leaves from the bulbs and cut the bulbs lengthwise into paper-thin slices. Cut off the ends from the endive heads. Cut most of the leaves in half lengthwise, leaving the remaining leaves whole for variety. Combine the fennel and Belgian endive in a bowl and toss gently.

Using a vegetable peeler, shave the cheese directly over the fennel and endive. Scatter the onion over as well. Drizzle with the dressing. Grind the green peppercorns in a mortar with a pestle or in a pepper mill, and sprinkle over the salad. Serve at once.

SALADS

Roasted Beet, Walnut, Gorgonzola, and Arugula Salad

Serves 4 to 6

Sweet beets come creeping out of obscurity when scattered atop arugula leaves and sprinkled with roasted walnuts and crumbly bits of Gorgonzola. This salad makes a great light lunch, or is lovely in combination with Celery Root Rémoulade (page 112) and Spicy Tunisian Carrot Salad with Caraway, Olives, and Feta (page 104).

2 pounds beets

4 cups arugula leaves or spinach leaves

$^1/_2$ cup walnut pieces

Dressing:

1 clove garlic, minced

1 teaspoon Dijon mustard

Salt and freshly ground pepper to taste

2 tablespoons balsamic vinegar

$^1/_3$ cup fruity extra-virgin olive oil, preferably French

$^1/_3$ cup crumbled Gorgonzola or other blue cheese (3 ounces)

Preheat an oven to 400 degrees F.

Remove the beet greens if still attached, leaving a $^1/_2$-inch-long stem; do not peel. Place the beets in a roasting pan with $^1/_2$ inch water. Roast until the beets can be easily pierced with a fork, about 1 hour. Remove from oven. (Alternatively, place the beets in a saucepan with boiling water to cover and cook at a slow, rolling boil until tender, 45 minutes to 1 hour; drain.) When cool enough to handle, using a small, sharp knife, peel off the skins from the beets. Slice the beets into thin julienne strips and place in a bowl. Place the arugula or spinach leaves in a separate bowl.

In a small skillet over a medium heat, toast the walnut pieces for a few minutes, shaking the pan continuously to bring out the flavor of the nuts. Remove from the heat and set aside.

To make the dressing, whisk together all the dressing ingredients. Add half of the dressing to the arugula (or spinach) and toss to coat the leaves.

Arrange the leaves on a serving platter, covering the bottom so that when you mound the beets on top, some of the greens will remain visible. Toss the beets with the remaining dressing and mound on top of the leaves. Distribute the walnuts and crumbled Gorgonzola over the top. Serve at once.

Summer Fruit Salad with Minty Vinaigrette

Serves 6 to 8

Every summer when peaches, berries, melons, plums, and other seasonal fruits flourished, my mother made this salad. Now, when I make the salad each summer, memories of long, warm lunches on our deck come to mind. You may assemble your own selection of fruits according to what is in the market. The vinaigrette plays off the sweetness of the fruits. The salad goes well with an assortment of ripe cheeses and freshly baked bread.

Salad:

2 peaches, peeled, pitted, and sliced

2 nectarines, pitted and sliced

4 plums, pitted and sliced

4 apricots, pitted and sliced

1/2 pint blueberries

1/2 pint blackberries

1/2 pint raspberries

1/2 cantaloupe, seeded, peeled, and cut into bite-sized pieces

1/2 honeydew, seeded, peeled, and cut into bite-sized pieces

1/2 papaya, seeded, peeled, and cut into bite-sized pieces

1 mango, pitted, peeled, and cut into small pieces

1/2 cup each seedless red and green grapes

Dressing:

2 tablespoons balsamic vinegar

1/4 cup fruity extra-virgin olive oil

Salt and freshly ground pepper to taste

1/3 cup fresh mint leaves, cut into julienne strips

A few fresh mint sprigs for decoration

Prepare all the fruits as directed, peeling and cutting them over a large bowl to capture all the juices. Place the cut fruits and berries in the bowl.

To make the dressing, in a small bowl, whisk together all the ingredients. Pour the dressing over the fruits and toss gently with your hands. Garnish with the mint sprigs. Serve immediately, or cover and chill until serving.

Vegetables

Fried Capers

Makes About ⅓ cup

Use these crisp capers on top of pasta, in salads, with calves' liver (as it used to be served at the Four Seasons Restaurant in New York), or on grilled dishes.

⅓ cup salt-cured capers

¼ cup bulk extra-virgin olive oil

To reduce their saltiness, soak the capers in cold water to cover for 5 minutes, drain, rinse under cold water, and pat dry on paper towels.

In a small, heavy skillet over medium-high heat, warm the olive oil for 1 minute. Carefully drop the capers into the hot oil; the oil will splatter. Cook until they start to brown, about 2 minutes. Remove with a slotted spoon to paper towels to drain. If left uncovered, the capers will stay very crisp for a few hours. Eat them the day you cook them, however. They do not retain their crispiness.

Fried Leek Crisps

Serves 4

Used as a garnish, these crispy leek shreds add texture and flavor to grilled fish, salads, or pasta.

1 leek, about ½ pound

About ⅓ cup bulk extra-virgin olive oil

Salt and freshly ground pepper to taste

Trim the leek, leaving 3 inches of the green. Slice the leek in half lengthwise, then in half across the center. Rinse well in a basin of water. Cut the pieces into julienne strips ¼ inch wide by 3 inches long. Dry thoroughly on kitchen towels.

In a small skillet, pour in the olive oil to a depth of ½ inch. Heat to 365 degrees F. Add one-third of the leeks and agitate them with tongs or a fork so they don't burn.

When the strips are brown, after about 30 seconds, remove them with the tongs to a wire rack placed over paper towels. Season with salt and pepper to taste. Repeat with the remaining leeks.

Serve immediately, or recrisp in a 325 degree F oven for a few minutes.

OLIVE OIL • FROM TREE TO TABLE

Fritto Misto
Serves 4

One rainy spring night in Florence, I missed my train for a long-awaited trip to southern Italy. Luckily, my friends knew just what to do when they saw how disappointed I was. They brought me to a trattoria along the road to Greve-in-Chianti where we were staying, and ordered a big plate of *fritto misto* to begin. One bite and we canceled our veal chops and ordered two more helpings of *fritto misto*.

An inexpensive, bulk-grade extra-virgin or virgin oil may be used for frying (see page 34-35 for deep-frying instructions). Use a deep-fat thermometer with a heavy saucepan or a deep, heavy skillet, or a deep-fat fryer equipped with a thermostat. Any combination of vegetables will work. Here is a selection that works for four people as a main course.

4 small artichokes

1 lemon

1 eggplant, unpeeled, halved lengthwise, and thinly sliced crosswise

1 russet potato, unpeeled, cut into ¼-inch-thick slices

1 head radicchio, cut through the stem end into eighths

1 fennel bulb, trimmed and thinly sliced lengthwise

½ head cauliflower, core removed and thinly sliced crosswise

4 eggs

1 cup fine dried bread crumbs or semolina flour

Bulk extra-virgin or virgin olive oil for deep-frying

Lemon slices

Salt and freshly ground pepper for serving

To prepare the artichokes, fill a bowl with water and squeeze in the juice of the lemon, then throw in the lemon halves. Working with 1 artichoke at a time, trim off the bottom ½ inch of the stem, cut off the prickly tops, and cut the artichoke in half lengthwise. Pull off the dark, tough outer leaves and, with the tip of a small, sharp knife, cut out and discard the choke. Cut the artichoke in quarters. Drop the quarters into the lemon water. When all the artichokes have been cut, bring a saucepan filled with water to a boil. Drain the artichokes, add them to the boiling water, and cook until tender when pierced with a fork, about 3 minutes. Drain and pat dry.

Prepare the other vegetables as directed. Arrange all of the sliced vegetables on a platter. In a shallow dish, beat the eggs until blended. In another shallow dish, put the bread crumbs or semolina flour.

Preheat an oven to 200 degrees F for keeping the fried vegetables warm. Select one of the utensils described in the introduction and pour olive oil into it to a depth of 2½ inches. Heat to 350 to 365 degrees F. Working with a few vegetable slices at a time, dip them first into the egg, allowing excess egg to drop off, and then into the bread crumbs or flour, tapping off the excess. Add to the hot oil. Do not add too many pieces at one time, or the oil temperature will drop and the vegetables will absorb too much oil and become soggy. Fry, turning as needed, until golden brown, 3 to 5 minutes. Using tongs, remove to a wire rack placed over paper towels to drain. Repeat with the remaining vegetables, placing the drained vegetables on a serving platter in the oven to keep warm. Serve immediately with lots of sliced lemon and salt and pepper placed alongside.

Caramelized Roasted Vegetables

Serves 6 to 8

This dish is a wonderful accompaniment to roasted chicken or any meat or fish, and it is a hearty vegetarian main course. You can integrate whatever is in season, whatever catches your eye at the market. If peppers are out of season, omit them. If they are readily available, use more, perhaps even a combination of red, orange, and yellow. This is a freeform, rustic dish.

My friend Susan Andrews introduced me to this method of separating vegetables into two or three baking dishes so they are not crowded and have a chance to become crispy and brown. If you use a glazed terra-cotta baking dish, the vegetables will take about 1¼ hours to cook. In a glass dish they will take a little over an hour, and in a cast-iron skillet the roasting time will be only about 50 minutes. You can also use roasting pans or baking sheets.

1 sweet potato, peeled and cut into ½-inch-thick slices

1 russet potato, unpeeled, cut into ½-inch-thick slices

2 green zucchini, cut into ¾-inch-thick slices

2 yellow zucchini or summer squash, cut into ¾-inch-thick slices

1 eggplant, cubed, salted, allowed to drain for 30 minutes in a colander, and patted dry

1 head garlic, unpeeled and broken into cloves

2 yellow onions, cut into 8 wedges each

1 fennel bulb, trimmed and sliced into wedges

1 or more red bell peppers, seeded and cut lengthwise into ½-inch-wide strips

½ cup extra-virgin olive oil

Salt and freshly ground pepper to taste

2 fresh rosemary sprigs, or 1 tablespoon dried rosemary

Preheat an oven to 400 degrees F.

Arrange all the vegetables in 3 or more pans, drizzle with the olive oil, and sprinkle with salt and pepper. Using your hands, toss the vegetables so that all of them are evenly coated. Break up 1 of the rosemary sprigs and distribute it over the vegetables, or sprinkle the dried rosemary over them.

Roast until the vegetables are brown and tender, depending upon the baking vessel used (see introduction) and the size and variety of the vegetables. Transfer to a large platter and serve immediately with a sprig of rosemary on top.

VEGETABLES

Oven-roasted Asparagus
Serves 4

Something magic happens to vegetables when they are roasted. Their flavors sweeten and intensify. This method takes about the same time as steaming, but it is easier and the results are tastier.

1 pound slender to medium asparagus, tough ends broken off

3 tablespoons extra-virgin olive oil

1 tablespoon balsamic vinegar

Salt and freshly ground pepper to taste

¼ cup grated Parmesan cheese

Preheat an oven to 500 degrees F.

In a glass baking dish, arrange the asparagus in a single layer. Drizzle with the olive oil. Roast for 10 minutes. Test 1 spear; if it is not tender, roast for a minute or two longer. If it is tender, dribble the vinegar into the dish and shake the dish so that all the asparagus are coated with both the oil and vinegar. Season with salt and pepper. Using tongs so that most of the oil drips off, transfer the asparagus to a platter. Sprinkle with Parmesan. Serve immediately or at room temperature.

Grilled Radicchio and Belgian Endive
Serves 4 to 6

Brushed with olive oil, radicchio and endive can be grilled alongside other vegetables, a fish fillet, a roasted chicken, or a piece of grilled meat, or they can be prepared on their own as a starter. Traviso radicchio is the long, slender variety and is best for grilling, but round Chioggia radicchio can be used if that is all that is available.

6 Belgian endives

3 small heads radicchio (see introduction)

Extra-virgin olive oil for brushing

2 long fresh rosemary sprigs

Salt and freshly ground pepper to taste

Prepare a fire in a charcoal grill.

Cut the endive and radicchio heads in half lengthwise. Bring a large saucepan of salted water to a boil. Add the vegetables in batches and boil for 1 minute. Remove with a slotted spoon or tongs and drain well. Pat dry.

Brush the vegetables with olive oil and place on the grill rack about 6 inches above the fire. Grill, turning once and brushing with olive oil-dipped rosemary sprigs, until crisp-tender, about 5 minutes on each side. Transfer to a platter, sprinkle with salt and pepper, and serve.

Baked Tuscan White Beans

Makes 6 to 8 cups; serves 6 to 8

The hearths of many Tuscan farmhouses have andirons with extending ring braces for holding glass containers in which beans are slowly cooked. I enjoyed white beans slow-cooked at the end of a long day during the olive harvest at Borro al Fumo in Lecchi-in-Chianti, at the farmhouse of Charles Ewell and Nancy Leszczynski. The dish had been assembled early in the morning so it would be ready when everyone returned from the olive grove, tired and hungry.

Italian canned white beans are delicious and can be used to prepare a simple version of the dish we ate that night. Pour them into an earthenware dish with their juices and add fresh sage, salt, and pepper. Place in a 350 degree F oven until hot, and serve with a cruet of good Tuscan extra-virgin olive oil on the side, so everyone can drizzle on oil to their liking. Or you can make white baked beans from scratch using the following recipe, and serve with a salad and a good Chianti. You can also offer it as a side dish or spoon it onto crusty toast for a starter.

$2\frac{1}{2}$ cups dried *cannellini* beans, picked over and rinsed

3 cloves garlic

1 yellow onion, quartered

2 carrots, peeled and quartered crosswise

3 celery stalks, trimmed and quartered crosswise

3 bay leaves

6 to 8 fresh sage leaves, or 2 tablespoons dried sage

Salt and freshly ground pepper to taste

Extra-virgin olive oil for drizzling

Place the rinsed beans in a bowl and add water to cover by 3 inches (8 to 10 cups). Let stand overnight.

The next day, preheat an oven to 350 degrees F.

Drain the beans and place in a 4- to 5-quart earthenware or other oven-proof casserole. Add the whole garlic cloves, onion, carrots, celery, bay leaves, and sage leaves. Add water to cover by 3 inches (8 to 10 cups). Cover and bake until beans are tender, $1\frac{1}{2}$ to 2 hours. Check from time to time and add more water if it is fully absorbed before the beans are done.

Remove from the oven and remove the garlic, onion, carrots, celery, and bay leaves (or leave the vegetables in, if you like). Drain off a little liquid if the beans are too soupy, and then season with salt and pepper. Pour a little extra-virgin olive oil on top, or serve with a cruet of extra-virgin olive oil at the table. Store any leftovers, well covered, in the refrigerator for up to 3 days.

Variation: Drain cooked beans of juices and vegetables. Arrange in a layer on a baking dish, drizzle with olive oil, and sprinkle with 1 tablespoon of rosemary. Bake at 400 degrees F for 10 minutes, and serve alongside grilled fish.

Long-roasted Tomatoes
Serves 4

These tomatoes are sweeter than sugar, and savory with oil and salt—a classic accompaniment to roasted meats and fish.

$^1/_3$ cup extra-virgin olive oil

18 ripe plum or other small, ripe tomatoes

3 cloves garlic, minced

2 tablespoons dried oregano or herbes de Provence

Salt and freshly ground pepper to taste

Preheat an oven to 325 degrees F. Oil a 9-by-13-by-2-inch glass baking dish with a little of the olive oil.

Cut the tomatoes in half and place in the baking dish cut side up. Sprinkle evenly with the garlic and oregano or herbes de Provence. Drizzle with the remaining olive oil. Crowd the tomatoes, as they will shrink during cooking.

Bake the tomatoes until they are slightly shriveled and very sweet, about 1$^1/_2$ hours. During the cooking, baste the tomatoes with the olive oil in the dish a few times so they do not dry out. Remove from the oven and, using a slotted spatula, transfer the tomatoes to a serving plate, holding them over the baking dish to allow most of the oil to drip off. Season with salt and pepper. The leftover oil is great for dipping with bread. Serve hot or at room temperature.

Roasted Ratatouille

Serves 6 to 8

Provençal ratatouille is a lovely late summer and fall dish that can be made with ingredients fresh from the farmers' market, your own garden, or from any source that supplies juicy, ripe tomatoes, a splashy array of colored peppers, and firm, bright squash. This is a grilled version of a dish that is often sautéed. When the grilled ingredients are combined, the result is almost a vegetable jam, yet the ingredients stand up to one another, resulting in a slightly smoky dish with a dense, rich, layered flavor. Cook the vegetables over a medium-hot charcoal fire or over medium heat on a stove-top grill. Lightly oil the grill before starting.

Olives and capers that linger too long in a hot dish tend to become bitter, so add them after the vegetables have cooled. The same goes for the late addition of chopped basil and parsley, which will stay brighter and fresher if added just before serving. This dish is typically served at room temperature, but if you are in a rush, serve it warm, adding the last four ingredients at the very last possible minute. You can use more or less olive oil than indicated. Ratatouille is great with a sour baguette or as a side dish.

2 pounds globe or Asian eggplants, unpeeled, cut into $1\frac{1}{2}$-inch cubes

Salt

Splash of water

3 to 4 medium zucchini, a mixture of yellow and green, cut into long strips, $\frac{1}{2}$ inch thick

2 onions, preferably torpedo or red, cut into thin wedges

8 or more cloves garlic

About $\frac{1}{2}$ cup extra-virgin olive oil, preferably French

Freshly ground pepper to taste

3 or 4 bell peppers, in a mixture of colors

5 tomatoes, preferably a mixture of red, yellow, and orange

3 tablespoons chopped fresh basil

3 tablespoons chopped fresh Italian parsley

2 tablespoons salt-cured capers, rinsed and drained (optional)

12 to 16 Niçoise olives, pitted and chopped (optional)

Fruity extra-virgin olive oil for serving (optional)

Prepare a fire in a charcoal grill and let burn down to a medium-hot fire, or preheat a stove-top grill over medium heat.

In a bowl, toss the cubed eggplant with a sprinkling of salt and the water, transfer to a colander, cover with a plate weighted with a heavy can or brick, and let stand for about 1 hour to press out any moisture and bitterness.

Meanwhile, combine the zucchini, onions, and garlic cloves in a bowl with about 1 tablespoon of the olive oil and toss well. Transfer to the oiled grill rack or stove-top grill and grill, turning as necessary, until the zucchini and onion are tender and branded with grill marks. Grill the garlic cloves until golden, taking care not to let them fall through the cracks if using a charcoal grill. Sprinkle all the vegetables with a little salt and pepper. Transfer the vegetables to a bowl when done, allowing them to cool, then cut into bite-sized pieces.

Place the peppers on the grill rack or stove-top grill and grill, turning as needed, until the skins are blackened, or blacken them over a flame on a gas stove. Transfer to a bowl, and cover snugly with a kitchen towel. When cool enough to handle, peel off the skin. Remove the stems and seeds and cut lengthwise into narrow strips. Set aside in a bowl, drizzle with a splash of the olive oil, and sprinkle them with salt and pepper.

Drain the eggplant cubes, pat dry, and toss in a bowl with a few tablespoons of the olive oil. Place on the grill rack or stove-top grill and grill until tender and browned. Add to the zucchini-garlic-onion mixture. Season with salt and pepper.

Hold the tomatoes over the flame on a gas stove to blacken the skin, or submerge into a saucepan filled with boiling water for 15 to 30 seconds, then plunge into cold water. Using a small, sharp knife, remove the skin and core from each tomato. Cut each tomato in half, place each half in the palm of your hand, and squeeze out the seeds. Slice the tomato halves into small wedges.

In a large saucepan over medium heat, warm a few tablespoons of olive oil. Add the tomato wedges and cook until tender, about 10 minutes. Add the eggplant mixture and the bell peppers and cook, turning gently until mixed, for 10 minutes longer until almost a jam. Using a slotted spoon, transfer the vegetables to a serving bowl and let cool. If a lot of liquid remains in the pan, place it over medium heat and cook until reduced by half, then pour it back over the cooling mixture.

Just before serving, stir in the basil, parsley, and the capers and olives, if using. Taste and adjust the seasonings. You may want to add more olive oil at this point, or you can serve a very good French or mild fruity olive oil on the side.

Spring Green Vegetable Stew with Shaved Pecorino

Serves 6 to 8

During the spring, ingredients for this dish come into the markets all over the Mediterranean. Each region in each country welcomes the season with its own version of a "green stew." I was delighted by this stew, called *scaffata*, when I visited Italy's largest olive oil–producing region, Apulia, early one May. The food there is light, colorful, and largely vegetable based. Use any combination of the following vegetables or all of them. A fine green Tuscan oil would be lovely threaded over all. While a good Apulian oil would also be welcome, such oils are generally exported to Tuscany, where they are packed and labeled as products of that region.

1 pound fava beans

1 lemon

10 to 16 baby artichokes, approximately 2 ounces each

1 ¹/₂ pounds asparagus

¹/₂ pound sugar snap peas, strings removed, or 1 cup shelled English peas

1 fennel bulb

Dressing:

¹/₃ cup extra-virgin olive oil, preferably Tuscan

Splash of balsamic vinegar

2 tablespoons minced shallots

1 teaspoon Dijon mustard

Pinch of red pepper flakes

Salt and freshly ground pepper to taste

¹/₃ pound pecorino or Parmesan cheese

¹/₂ cup fresh mint leaves, cut into julienne strips

To shell the fava beans, remove the beans as you would peas from a pod. Bring a saucepan filled with water to a boil, add the favas, and blanch for 1 minute. Drain and immerse the favas in cold water to retain their color. Drain again and slip the skin off each fava bean. If the beans are very small and tender, you need not peel them. Set aside.

Fill a bowl with water and squeeze in the juice from the lemon, then throw in the lemon halves. Remove at least three layers of outer leaves from the artichokes to reach the light green interior leaves. Working with 1 artichoke at a time, trim off the dark spot where the artichoke was attached to the bush and the pointed top 1 inch of the leaves. Cut in half lengthwise and immediately drop the slices into the lemon water.

Bring a saucepan filled with water to a boil. Meanwhile, snap off the tough ends of the asparagus, and cut the spears on the diagonal into 3-inch lengths. Place in a colander or steamer basket that fits snugly over the pot of boiling water, cover, and steam until just tender, 3 to 5 minutes. Remove from the pan and immediately rinse under running cold water to halt the cooking and preserve the bright green color. Drain well and set aside.

Bring another saucepan filled with water to a boil. Add the snap peas or English peas and cook for 1 minute. Drain and rinse immediately under running cold water to halt the cooking and preserve the bright green color. Drain well and set aside.

Trim off the feathery tops and stalks from the fennel bulb. Cut off any bruised leaves from the bulb and cut lengthwise into paper- thin slices.

130

To make the dressing, in a small bowl, whisk together all the ingredients. Drain the artichokes and pat dry. Scatter the artichokes, asparagus, peas, and fennel on a large platter with a shallow rim. Drizzle on the dressing and toss well. Using a vegetable peeler, shave the cheese over the top and then sprinkle on the mint. Serve at room temperature.

Note: *You can ready all the vegetables up to a few hours in advance, but do not drain the artichokes until serving time, or they will discolor. Do not add the dressing to the other vegetables until just before serving, or they will begin to discolor as well. Instead, drizzle the vegetables with a little olive oil to keep them moist.*

Spinach with Pine Nuts and Raisins

Serves 2 to 4

Here is a classic dish that is eaten with only minor variations in Greece, Sicily and other parts of Italy, Spain, and France. Raisins are a tasty antidote to the slightly metallic notes that spinach sometimes has.

¼ cup golden raisins

Boiling water to cover

2 to 3 tablespoons pine nuts

2 tablespoons extra-virgin olive oil

3 cloves garlic, chopped

1 pound spinach, carefully rinsed, drained, and chopped

Salt and and freshly ground pepper to taste

Fresh lemon juice and extra-virgin olive oil if serving at room temperature

Place the raisins in a small bowl and add boiling water to cover. Allow to stand for 10 minutes until the raisins are plump, then drain.

Meanwhile, in a small skillet over medium heat, toast the pine nuts, stirring constantly, for 1 to 2 minutes to bring out their flavor and give them a bit of crunch. Remove from the heat and set aside.

In a 12-inch skillet over medium heat, warm the olive oil. Add the garlic and sauté for 1 minute. Add the spinach a little at a time, adding more as each batch begins to wilt. Cook, stirring constantly, until all the spinach has wilted, 3 to 5 minutes. Pour the raisins over the spinach, season with salt and pepper, and mix well.

Using a slotted spoon, transfer the spinach to a serving dish, discarding the liquid in the pan, and sprinkle the pine nuts over the top. Serve immediately. Or serve at room temperature with a squeeze of lemon juice and a drizzle of olive oil.

132

Sweet-and-Sour Small Onions
Serves 4

Here is a recipe from L'Osteria del Forno on Columbus Avenue in San Francisco's Italian North Beach neighborhood. It is called *cipolline en agrodolce* and is made with small, flat, sweet onions. The dish is good on its own or as an accompaniment to meat or fowl.

1 pound *cipolline* onions (see introduction)

¼ cup balsamic vinegar

1 tablespoon sugar

½ tablespoon salt

2 tablespoons extra-virgin olive oil

1 teaspoon chopped fresh oregano

Immerse the onions in a bowl with chilled water to cover for a few minutes to loosen their skins, then peel them with a small, sharp knife.

Put the onions in a large pan with water to a depth of 2 inches. Place over medium heat, bring to a simmer, and cook, uncovered, for 15 minutes. If the water evaporates, add more as needed to keep the onions covered. Stir in the vinegar, sugar, and salt. Reduce the heat to low and simmer for 1 hour, adding more water if necessary.

Transfer to a serving plate with any pan juices, and let cool to room temperature. Drizzle with the olive oil, sprinkle with the oregano, and serve.

Mashed Potatoes with Celery Root and Horseradish
Serves 2 to 4

Try this new twist on mashed potatoes, in which celery root and fresh horseradish join the favorite tuber. Serve with a roasted leg of lamb, fish, or fowl.

1 celery root, about ¾ pound, peeled and quartered

4 russet potatoes, peeled and quartered

4 pieces fresh horseradish root, each 1 inch square, peeled

Salt and white pepper to taste

¼ to ⅓ cup extra-virgin olive oil, preferably mild and sweet

In a heavy saucepan, combine the celery root, potatoes, and horseradish. Add water just to cover and bring to a boil. Reduce the heat to medium and cook until the ingredients are soft. They will take different amounts of time to cook; the horseradish will be the last to soften. As the potatoes and celery root are ready, remove them with a slotted spoon and keep warm. Then drain the horseradish pieces when they are done.

Transfer the vegetables to a bowl and mash with a potato masher, or pass through a food mill into a bowl. Stir in the salt and white pepper and drizzle with the olive oil. Serve immediately.

Tattooed Potatoes with Rosemary

Serves 4 to 6

I had these potatoes for Christmas dinner at the home of my friend Lindita Klein. She found a similar recipe in *Gourmet* magazine that called for butter in place of the olive oil and a sprig of Italian parsley in place of the rosemary. You can use either or both of the herbs, but olive oil makes these potatoes remarkable. This is one of those dishes that everyone loves and wants to know how to make. It is simple and enormously appealing.

$\frac{1}{3}$ to $\frac{1}{2}$ cup extra-virgin olive oil

1 teaspoon salt

$\frac{1}{2}$ teaspoon freshly cracked pepper

6 small fresh rosemary sprigs or Italian parsley leaves

3 russet potatoes, unpeeled, cut in half lengthwise

Preheat an oven to 400 degrees F.

Pour the olive oil into a medium-sized glass baking dish and add the salt and pepper. Stir to combine. Press a rosemary sprig or parsley leaf on the cut side of each potato half and place cut side down in the oil.

Bake until the potatoes are nicely browned, 40 to 45 minutes. While the potatoes are cooking, using a spatula, gently move them every now and then to keep them from sticking. When they are ready, remove them from the pan, turning them flat side up and carefully leaving the pressed herb in place. Arrange on a platter and serve immediately.

Note: *A glass dish works well in this case because you can check for doneness by carefully holding the dish overhead and looking to see if the potatoes are browned. When you do this, be careful not to spill the hot oil. A metal pan will do, too, but testing for doneness will not be as easy.*

Sauces

Two Charmoula Sauces

Charmoula is an addictive Moroccan sauce that will brighten almost any fish or vegetable dish. It is typically used as a fish marinade, but it is also wonderful on grilled eggplant slices. I like it with sea bass baked in parchment, on grilled ahi tuna, or even on roasted chicken breasts. But for the chicken, Moroccan cook Bouchaid Fattah makes a variation, also called charmoula, that he learned from his mother in Casablanca. Both sauces are rich, aromatic, and delicious; they are so very different, however, that it is hard to believe they both have the same name.

Make sure your spices—cumin, mild (sweet) paprika, and hot paprika—have not been on the shelf too long. Their flavors diminish over time.

Charmoula I
Makes about 1 cup; serves 4

2 cloves garlic, finely chopped

1 teaspoon ground cumin

1 teaspoon mild paprika

Pinch of hot paprika

1 cup chopped fresh Italian parsley

1 cup chopped fresh cilantro

3 tablespoons fresh lemon juice

Shredded zest of 1 lemon

1/2 to 3/4 cup extra-virgin olive oil

Salt to taste

Combine all the ingredients in a bowl and mix well. Allow the flavors to mingle for about 1 hour before serving. This sauce is best made by hand; it is not as bright and textured if made in a food processor.

Charmoula II

Makes about 2 cups; serves 6

1 green bell pepper

1 red bell pepper

¼ cup extra-virgin olive oil

1 white onion, chopped

4 cloves garlic, minced

Splash of water

1 teaspoon ground cumin

1 teaspoon mild paprika

Pinch of hot paprika or
   cayenne pepper

½ teaspoon ground ginger

12 pitted, sliced imported
   green olives

¾ cup finely chopped cilantro
   leaves

¾ cup finely chopped Italian
   parsley leaves

Roast the peppers over the flame of a gas stove or in a broiler until the skins are blackened and blistered. Put them in a bowl and cover snugly with a kitchen towel. When cool enough to handle, peel off the skins, cut in half lengthwise, and remove and discard the stems and seeds. Cut into 1-inch squares.

In a large skillet over medium heat, warm the olive oil. Add the onion and sauté until translucent, 3 to 5 minutes. Add the garlic and cook for 1 minute longer. Add the roasted peppers, reduce the heat to low, and then add the water. Cook gently for 5 minutes longer. Add the cumin, both paprikas (or cayenne), and the ginger, and continue to simmer for about 5 minutes longer, to integrate the flavors. Stir in the olives and remove from the heat. Transfer to a bowl, add the cilantro and parsley, and stir to combine.

Spiced Orange Mayonnaise

Makes about 2 ½ cups

This Moroccan-inspired mayonnaise is good with fish that is not too delicate, such as salmon or swordfish.

1 cup fresh orange juice

3 egg yolks

Juice of ½ lemon

1 ½ cups mild extra-virgin olive oil

Salt and freshly ground pepper

Pinch each of ground cumin, cloves, and allspice

In a sauté pan over medium heat, simmer the orange juice until it is reduced to ⅓ cup, about 10 minutes. Remove from heat and let cool.

Place a stainless-steel bowl on a folded kitchen towel (so it won't slide) and add the egg yolks and lemon juice to it. Whisk until smooth. Add the olive oil drop by drop at first, and then in a very slow, steady stream once the mixture starts to emulsify. Whisk until it becomes thick. Then add the spices and orange juice a little at a time, whisking until combined.

Alternatively, use a food processor or blender: Combine the egg yolks and lemon juice and pulse until smooth. With the motor running, add the olive oil in a thin, steady stream. Process until the mixture starts to thicken. Then add the spices and orange juice a little at a time, combining well.

Transfer the mayonnaise to a bowl or jar, cover tightly, and refrigerate for up to 5 days.

Mayonnaise
Makes about 1 cup

This recipe uses fewer eggs than a classic mayonnaise, which makes it lower in cholesterol. By adding garlic, you have aioli; by adding extra mustard, you have a lovely rémoulade to mix with blanched celery root; and by adding chopped parsley, you have a green sauce that tastes great with fish or sliced tomatoes. See variations for correct proportions.

2 teaspoons Dijon mustard

1 egg

Pinch of salt

Dash of white pepper

1 cup mild extra-virgin olive oil

2 tablespoons fresh lemon juice or white vinegar

Place a stainless-steel bowl on a folded kitchen towel (so it won't slide) and add the mustard, egg, salt, and white pepper to it. Whisk until smooth. Add the olive oil drop by drop at first, and then in a very slow, steady stream once the mixture starts to emulsify. Whisk until it becomes thick. Then add the lemon juice or vinegar a little at a time, whisking until combined.

Alternatively, use a food processor or blender: Combine the mustard, egg, salt, and white pepper. Pulse until blended and smooth. With the motor running, add the olive oil in a slow, thin, steady stream. Process until the mixture starts to thicken. Stop when all the oil has been added and scrape down the sides. Then add the lemon juice or vinegar a little at a time, combining well.

Transfer the mayonnaise to a bowl or jar, cover tightly, and refrigerate for up to 5 days.

Variations: To make aioli, add 1 tablespoon minced garlic after the salt. To make rémoulade, add 2 additional teaspoons Dijon mustard. To make green sauce, purée 1 cup finely chopped and mixed watercress and Italian parsley leaves with 1 tablespoon of the finished mayonnaise in a food processor, and then add the rest of the mayonnaise and pulse just until blended.

141

Onion Marmalade

Makes about 2 cups; serves 4 to 6

This slow-cooked savory marmalade is inspired by the *confit d'oignons* made by fine Basque chef Gerald Hirigoyen, who has two stunning restaurants, Fringale and Pastis, in San Francisco. Every time I go to Fringale, I order seared tuna with Hirigoyen's tender sweet-and-sour onion *confit*. This adaptation of his recipe is wonderful served on warm flat bread, in a sandwich with grilled sausage, or on a barbecued steak. It also makes a great present packed into a pretty jar.

2 slices pancetta, 2 ounces each, or $\frac{1}{4}$ pound bacon

$\frac{1}{4}$ cup extra-virgin olive oil, preferably French

2 large white onions, thinly sliced

$\frac{1}{2}$ cup balsamic vinegar

$\frac{1}{4}$ cup sherry vinegar

$\frac{1}{2}$ cup water

1 teaspoon salt

$\frac{1}{4}$ teaspoon white pepper

2 teaspoons sugar

Pinch of cayenne pepper

Cut the pancetta or bacon into $\frac{1}{2}$-inch dice. In a large, heavy skillet over medium-high heat, warm the olive oil. Add the pancetta or bacon and sauté until barely crisp, about 2 minutes. Add the onions and continue to cook, stirring frequently, until the onions are golden brown, 8 to 10 minutes.

Stir in both vinegars, the water, salt, white pepper, sugar, and cayenne. Bring to a slow boil over medium heat and boil gently, stirring often and scraping the bottom of the pan, until most of the liquid has evaporated, 10 to 12 minutes.

Remove from the heat and let cool completely, then pour off any excess liquid and transfer to a tightly capped jar. Store in the refrigerator for up to a few weeks. Bring to room temperature before serving.

Peperonata

Makes 5 to 6 cups; serves 6 to 8

A satisfying, sweet-and-sour (*agrodolce*) melding of peppers, tomatoes, and olives, this Italian sauce is good on roasted chicken breasts or grilled fish. With the addition of a little extra olive oil, it becomes a quick pasta sauce. Packed into a tightly capped container, it travels well. I like to bring it along on picnics or to parties to eat on flat bread or crackers. It is also tasty on grilled slices of country-style bread for *bruschetta*, or as a side dish with a little *ricotta salata* or feta cheese crumbled over the top.

3 pounds bell peppers (about 6), a mixture of red and yellow

¼ cup extra-virgin olive oil

1 red onion, minced

3 tablespoons red wine vinegar

6 medium-ripe tomatoes, peeled, seeded, and chopped, or 1 can (28 ounces) whole Italian plum tomatoes, drained and chopped

6 to 7 fresh basil leaves, chopped, or 1 teaspoon dried basil

12 Sicilian green olives, pitted and slivered (about ½ cup)

3 tablespoons salt-cured capers, rinsed and drained

Roast the peppers over the flame of a gas stove or in a broiler until the skins are blackened and blistered. Put them in a bowl and cover snugly with a kitchen towel. When cool enough to handle, peel off the skin, cut in half lengthwise, and remove and discard the stems and seeds. Cut into 1-inch squares.

In a large, heavy skillet over medium heat, warm the olive oil. Add the onion and sauté until translucent, 2 to 3 minutes. Add the vinegar and continue to cook for 1 minute. Add the tomatoes and cook, stirring occasionally, until most of their liquid has evaporated, 3 to 5 minutes. Add the peppers and simmer, stirring until the ingredients are well combined, 3 to 5 minutes longer. Stir in the basil, olives, and capers (they'll impart a bitter flavor if added earlier) and simmer for a few more minutes to blend the flavors.

Remove from the heat and serve at once, or let cool completely, pack in a tightly capped jar, and refrigerate. Keeps for at least 1 week.

Italian Green Sauce

Makes about 1 cup; serves 4 to 6

This piquant, raw green sauce, called *salsa verde*, is traditionally served with *bollito misto*, a dish of assorted boiled meats. It makes the rather plain flavors of the meats sparkle, and it is also delicious with grilled fish or chicken breasts. A similar green sauce, *gremolata* (page 93), calls for fewer anchovies and is not bound with bread crumbs.

2 slices day-old country-style bread

3 tablespoons salt-cured capers, rinsed and drained

4 oil-packed anchovy fillets, rinsed and chopped

3 or more cloves garlic, chopped

2 tablespoons fresh lemon juice

Grated zest of 1 lemon

⅓ to ½ cup extra-virgin olive oil, preferably Tuscan

2½ cups fresh Italian parsley leaves

Break up the bread and place in a food processor. Pulse to make coarse crumbs. Remove and set aside.

Add the capers, anchovy fillets, garlic, lemon juice, lemon zest, and olive oil to the processor and pulse to combine. Add the parsley leaves and process until smooth.

Transfer the contents of the processor to a bowl and add the bread crumbs. Stir to combine. Use immediately, or cover and store for up to 3 days.

Note: The sauce can also be made by hand: Crush the bread with a rolling pin between 2 kitchen towels. Chop the capers, anchovy fillets, garlic, and parsley by hand and combine with the bread crumbs. Stir in the lemon juice, zest, and olive oil, combining well.

144

Romesco Sauce

Makes about 2 cups; serves 6 to 8

Salsa romesco is the best-known of the Spanish almond-based sauces. Sometimes hazelnuts, pine nuts, or walnuts are added to provide extra flavor. The sauce is a wonderful accompaniment to vegetables or fish.

The first time I had this sauce was at a Catalonian meal one early spring. The table was decorated with small olive branches, hazelnuts, and acorns. Fresh rosemary branches were strewn on the tile floor of the dining room, so that when you walked to your chair, you crushed the limbs. They released a fragrance that mingled with the aroma, rising from huge platters of paella, steamed mussels and baby cockles, and *calcots*, young, white leek-like Tarragona onions, which are repeatedly covered with chalky soil when they are growing to keep them white and tender. But my favorite combination was a *romesco* sauce with a spring salad of escarole and fava beans.

Serve as a salad dressing thinned with a little more olive oil, as a sauce with fish, or a dip for vegetables.

2 large, dried, mild to mildly hot chilies such as *ancho* or *pasilla*, seeded

1 cup hot water

10 cloves garlic, chopped

1 yellow onion, chopped

2 medium-ripe tomatoes, peeled and seeded

¼ cup extra-virgin olive oil, preferably Spanish

12 hazelnuts

12 almonds

½ teaspoon salt

½ teaspoon red pepper flakes, or more to taste

2 tablespoons sherry vinegar or red wine vinegar

1 tablespoon finely chopped fresh Italian parsley

Preheat an oven to 400 degrees F.

In a bowl, combine the large chilies and the hot water and let stand for 20 minutes.

In a glass or ceramic baking dish, combine the garlic, onion, and tomatoes. Drizzle with the olive oil. Bake for 30 minutes until the ingredients have a roasted appearance and flavor.

Meanwhile, in a skillet over medium heat, toast the hazelnuts and almonds, shaking the pan continuously, until fragrant, about 2 minutes. Turn out onto a plate to cool for a few minutes.

In a mortar or a food processor, combine the salt, red pepper flakes, and the toasted nuts. Grind with a pestle or pulse in the food processor until a paste begins to form.

Drain and chop the soaked peppers, then add to the mortar or food processor. When the tomato mixture is ready, add it to the mortar or food processor as well, being sure to scrape out all of the olive oil from the dish. Grind or pulse together all of the ingredients until slightly thickened and smooth.

Add the vinegar and parsley and mix well to combine completely. Store in a tightly capped jar for up to 1 week in the refrigerator. Bring to room temperature before serving.

Skordalia
Makes 2 1/2 to 3 cups

Traditionally, this sensational Greek garlic sauce is used for fried fish such as calamari, but it complements grilled shrimp and other grilled fish and shellfish as well. It's also good with vegetables—eggplant, beets, zucchini, asparagus, cauliflower, tomatoes—and with rabbit or chicken.

The sauce is best made in a mortar with a pestle. Bread is sometimes used in place of the potatoes; walnuts or blanched and toasted almonds can stand in for the pine nuts. Skordalia is a lovely, dense pungent sauce; it is not for the timid eater.

2 tablespoons pine nuts

3 to 5 cloves garlic

1/4 teaspoon salt

2 cups hot mashed potatoes (about 3 large potatoes)

1/2 cup extra-virgin olive oil, preferably Greek

About 1/4 cup fresh lemon juice or distilled white vinegar

Salt and white pepper to taste

In a small skillet over medium heat, toast the pine nuts, stirring constantly, for 1 to 2 minutes to bring out their flavor and give them a bit of crunch. Remove from the heat and let cool.

In a mortar, combine the garlic, salt, and pine nuts and grind with a pestle until they become a paste.

Add the potatoes and mash with the pestle until the mixture is smooth. In a slow, steady stream, pour in the olive oil, as if you are making mayonnaise. Add the lemon juice or vinegar a little at a time, tasting as you go. The sauce should be thick and smooth. Season with salt and white pepper. Let stand at room temperature for 1 hour before serving to allow the flavors to deepen. Any leftover sauce can be stored tightly covered in a refrigerator for up to a few days.

Three Vinaigrettes

My father was the vinaigrette maker in our family. One Christmas, the rest of us gave him a fancy cruet with lines etched on the glass indicating the levels to which the vinegar and oil should be poured. He'd add Colman's dry mustard, a dash each of Tabasco and Worcestershire sauce, salt, pepper, Italian red wine vinegar, and Bertolli olive oil. My mother, being a bit of a Francophile, always argued that Dijon was superior to dry mustard, and that the dressing should be mixed just before serving, never left on the shelf possibly to turn rancid. My brother, a very good cook, believes in salting salad greens, barely coating them with oil, and then splashing in a hint of vinegar. He then tastes the mixture, and adjusts the acid-oil balance accordingly.

I learned how to make my salad dressing in France from my friend Caroline DuCroq. She chops a couple of shallots, adds them to a medium-sized bowl, drops in a tablespoon of Dijon mustard, salt, and pepper and whisks them together until an emulsion starts to form. Then she adds a splash of the best red wine or balsamic vinegar, and next, with one hand, whisks as she drizzles in about half a cup of great olive oil. She tastes until it's just the way she remembers *her* father making it—slightly thick and creamy—the perfect dressing for fresh greens from the open-air markets of Paris.

I love to dress beets, carrots, celery root, colorful bell pepper strips, thinly sliced cucumbers, tomatoes, boiled potatoes, *salade niçoise*, rice salads, chicken salads, roast beef salads, and bread salads with this vinaigrette, or a variation on it. Sometimes I add capers, thinly sliced Bermuda onion, green onion, chopped hard-cooked egg, grated cheese, or anchovies—but never all at once. Keep it simple. Plain dressings are best. I love to taste the flavor and greenness of the lettuces. I always have assorted lettuces from the farmers' market, prewashed and ready to go, in my refrigerator—arugula, watercress, frisée, miner's lettuce, Belgian endive, parsley, and lately purslane. Keep in mind that if you dress asparagus or green beans with a vinaigrette, their green color may turn slightly gray.

Here are three vinaigrette recipes. Use different vinegars if you like, or if you really want the oil to stand out, try a mild-flavored *verjus* (made from grapes harvested when their acid levels are high and sugars are low) instead of the suggested vinegars.

Vinaigrette in a Salad Bowl
Makes about ½ cup

This is a typical French method for making a vinaigrette. It is put together at the last minute in the bowl—just add greens and toss. I always use my best olive oils for these vinaigrettes.

1 shallot, minced

Salt and freshly ground pepper to taste

1 teaspoon Dijon mustard

2 to 3 tablespoons red wine vinegar or balsamic vinegar

⅓ cup extra-virgin olive oil

In a salad bowl, combine the shallot, salt, pepper, and the mustard. With the back of a fork, mash them together. Add the vinegar and whisk well. Drizzle in the olive oil while whisking constantly.

Variation: Add 1 or 2 salt-cured anchovies, rinsed, filleted, and chopped, with the mustard.

Vinaigrette in a Jar
Makes about ¾ cup

You can play around with extra ingredients in this vinaigrette: more Tabasco and Worcestershire, some soy sauce, some fresh herbs, another type of vinegar, or even a pinch of dark brown sugar (especially if you've inadvertently added too much salt).

¼ cup, or slightly less, red wine vinegar

½ cup extra-virgin olive oil

1 teaspoon Dijon mustard

3 cloves garlic, chopped, or more or less to taste

Dash of Worcestershire sauce

Dash of Tabasco sauce

Salt and freshly ground pepper to taste

Combine all the ingredients in a tightly capped jar and shake well. The dressing will keep for a few days on a cool, dark shelf. You may not want to include the garlic if you plan to keep the dressing for a few days.

Quick Vinaigrette
Makes about ½ cup

My friends Linda Bucklin and Ruth Hunter each make wonderful salads. They claim it's because they use equal proportions of balsamic vinegar to olive oil. It seems a bit odd, but this dressing always works. Ruth Hunter adds Worcestershire sauce—a dash.

¼ cup balsamic vinegar

¼ cup extra-virgin olive oil

2 tablespoons Dijon mustard

3 cloves garlic, minced

Salt and freshly cracked pepper to taste

Whisk together all the ingredients and serve at once.

149

Breads & Sweets

Fennel–Olive Oil Quick Bread
Makes 1 loaf

This recipe comes from one of my favorite cooks, Nancy Barbour. It is quick and easy to make, and it tastes great dipped in olive oil.

3 cups self-rising flour

3 tablespoons light brown sugar

1 tablespoon crushed fennel seeds

2 tablespoons chopped fresh fennel tops, or 1 tablespoon dried dill

1 can (12 ounces) light beer

2 to 3 tablespoons extra-virgin olive oil

Preheat an oven to 375 degrees F. Oil a 9-by-5-inch loaf pan with olive oil.

In a bowl, combine the flour, brown sugar, fennel seeds, and fennel tops or dill. Add the beer and beat vigorously with a wooden spoon until well mixed.

Pour into the prepared loaf pan and pour the olive oil evenly over the top. Bake until the top is golden, 50 to 55 minutes. Carefully slip it out of the pan and tap it on the bottom; it should sound hollow. Turn out the loaf onto a wire rack to cool.

152

Black Olive and Olive Oil Bread

Makes 2 small loaves

This bread is a specialty of the Turks of Cyprus. It is adapted from *Classical Turkish Cooking* by Ayla Algar. The minty flavor mingles delightfully with the olives. The bread turns out best baked on a hot pizza stone or unglazed paver, but you can use a baking sheet, too. It keeps well, wrapped in plastic wrap, for a few days.

2 1/2 teaspoons active dry yeast (1 package)

Pinch of sugar

1 1/8 cups warm low-fat or skim milk (90 to 100 degrees F)

3 3/4 cups unbleached all-purpose flour, plus flour for work surface

1/2 cup finely chopped yellow onion

1/3 cup finely chopped fresh mint

1/3 cup extra-virgin olive oil, plus extra for oiling rising bowl

1 teaspoon salt

1 1/4 cups imported black olives, pitted and roughly chopped

Cornmeal for sprinkling

In a small bowl, dissolve the yeast and sugar in the warm milk and set aside until it begins to foam, 10 to 15 minutes.

Place the 3 3/4 cups flour in a large bowl and make a well in the center. Add the onion, mint, 1/3 cup olive oil, salt, olives, and yeast mixture to the well. Using your hands, mix together the ingredients until they form a ball.

Transfer the dough to a lightly floured work surface. Knead until smooth and somewhat spongy, 10 to 15 minutes. Gather the dough into a ball and place in a large oiled bowl. Cover the bowl with a kitchen towel or plastic wrap and set aside in a warm spot to rise until doubled in size, about 2 hours.

Punch down the dough and turn out onto a lightly floured work surface. Knead lightly and divide in half. Knead and fold each half into a small, tapered oval loaf that is wide at the center. Using a sharp knife, make a lengthwise slit down the center of each loaf. Transfer the loaves onto an inverted baking sheet (so they will easily slide off when ready to bake), cover with a damp kitchen towel, and let rise in a warm spot for about 2 hours.

Place a pizza stone (or 2 stones if you have them) in the middle of an oven and preheat to 450 degrees F for 30 minutes. Sprinkle the stone(s) with cornmeal. Slide a risen loaf onto the hot stone (or 1 loaf onto each stone). Reduce the heat to 400 degrees F and bake until the crust is a rich brown and crisp, 30 to 35 minutes. The crust will be tender with a pleasant crunch, and the interior will be moist. Transfer to a wire rack to cool, and repeat with the second loaf if you only have 1 stone.

Dried Fig Breakfast Bread

Makes 2 loaves

When I first visited Apulia in southern Italy, I was charmed by the locally made breads. I had huge, crusty wheels of country bread, smaller loaves with olives, pits and all, and I tasted lovely tomato loaves that had been baked in ancient wood-fired ovens. I was, time and again, reminded of a story in *The Italian Baker* by Carol Field about the Apulian reverence for bread. She tells a legend of how people are held in contempt for wasting even a crumb of *pane pugliese*. Such sinners are destined to end up in Purgatory for as many years as there were crumbs wasted. There, the sinner spends the time gathering those fallen crumbs with his or her eyelids. Be assured, I did not waste a crumb.

I longed for these breads when I returned home. At the San Francisco Ferry Plaza Farmers' Market, I found one that reminded me of what I had eaten in Italy. Week after week, I'd wait in a long line for this fig bread. Finally I got up the nerve to ask Michael and Mary Gassen of Noe Valley Bakery and Bread Company for their recipe. It turns out that Michael loved Fig Newtons as a boy, and often devoured toast spread with fig jam. When he first started baking, he thought, why not put figs in the bread rather than on it. This bread is so good you'll want to make two loaves. It is dense and freezes beautifully.

1 teaspoon active dry yeast

1/4 teaspoon sugar

1 3/4 cups warm water (90 to 100 degrees F)

1 pound dried Black Mission figs, stemmed and halved (Calimyrna or Adriatic figs are acceptable substitutes)

3 1/2 cups bread flour, plus flour for work surface

2 1/4 teaspoons salt

2 tablespoons extra-virgin olive oil, plus extra for oiling rising bowl

In a small bowl, dissolve the yeast and the sugar in the warm water and set aside until it begins to foam, 10 to 15 minutes.

Place the figs in a large mixing bowl. Add the 3 1/2 cups flour, the salt, and 2 tablespoons olive oil. Toss the ingredients together to combine them roughly.

When the yeast mixture has begun to foam, pour it over the fig-flour mixture. Mix the ingredients together with a wooden spoon until well combined and all the flour has been absorbed. The dough will appear very rough and tacky, and look somewhat like a choclate chip cookie dough (with figs instead of chocolate chips).

Transfer the dough to a large, well-oiled mixing bowl, cover with a kitchen towel, and let stand in a warm place for 1 to 1 1/2 hours. Its volume will increase by about one-third.

Turn out the dough onto a generously floured work surface and divide it into 2 equal parts. Roll each part into a cylinder (loaf shape) and place on a well-floured or parchment paper–lined baking sheet. Refrigerate the loaves, uncovered, until they have firmed up, about 2 hours.

Remove the loaves from the refrigerator and transfer to another floured or parchment-lined baking sheet. Reshape the loaves into squat, square loaves. Let them rise until warmth has returned to them and they have flattened slightly, about 2 hours in a warm spot. They will not increase in size significantly, unlike regular bread dough.

Place a pizza stone (or two stones if you have them) in the middle of an oven and preheat to 400 degrees F for 30 minutes. Slide a risen loaf onto the hot stone (or 1 loaf onto each stone) and spray generously with water from a mister. Bake until a rich brown color and firm to the touch, about 35 minutes. Transfer to a wire rack to cool, and repeat with the second loaf if you have only 1 stone.

Note: If you don't have a pizza stone, you can use a baking sheet, but the results will not be as good.

Hazelnut and Almond Biscotti

Makes about 2 dozen cookies

The inspiration for these crisp, nutty biscotti comes from Frantoio Restaurant in Mill Valley, California. They were served the final day of the olive pressing season—the day blood oranges, tangerines, and Meyer lemons were pressed with mild, ripe California olives to make a product called "O" Olive Oil. In Italy, the pressing of citrus in an olive press at the end of the season is said to cure the stones—to neutralize them while they rest for the new harvest the following fall.

Replacing a few tablespoons of the olive oil in the recipe with olive oil crushed with citrus would add an interesting dimension to these biscotti. Although these Tuscan cookies are twice baked, according to tradition, the olive oil keeps them from becoming too hard. They are wonderful, after dinner, dipped into a glass of Vin Santo.

3/4 cup almonds

3/4 cup hazelnuts

2 large oranges

3 cups all-purpose flour

1 1/2 cups sugar

1 teaspoon baking powder

1/2 teaspoon baking soda

1/2 teaspoon salt

3 whole eggs

2 egg yolks

1/2 teaspoon vanilla extract

1/2 cup mild extra-virgin olive oil

Preheat an oven to 350 degrees F. Oil 2 baking sheets with olive oil.

In a heavy skillet over medium heat, combine the almonds and hazelnuts and toast, shaking the pan continuously, until fragrant, 1 to 2 minutes. Transfer the nuts to a food processor and pulse to break them up and release their flavor. Alternatively, chop by hand. Place in a large bowl.

Using the medium holes of a grater, remove the zest from the oranges and add to the nuts. Add the flour, sugar, baking powder, baking soda, and salt and mix with a wooden spoon. Then add the whole eggs, egg yolks, vanilla, and olive oil to the bowl and mix well.

Transfer the dough to a floured work surface and divide it into 4 equal portions. Using your palms, shape each portion into a log 10 inches long and 2 inches in diameter. Lay the logs lengthwise on the prepared baking sheets, leaving at least 2 inches between the logs. Do not crowd them as they will spread a little during baking. With the palm of your hand, flatten the logs slightly.

Bake until barely firm to the touch, about 25 minutes. Remove from the oven and let cool for 15 minutes. Using a large metal spatula, transfer to a cutting board. Cut the logs on the diagonal into slices 1 1/2 inches thick. Return to the baking sheets cut side down. Return to the oven.

Reduce the heat to 325 degrees F and bake until firm and almost crisp, 10 to 15 minutes longer. Transfer to wire racks to cool. The cookies will keep for a few weeks in an airtight container.

156

Polenta Coins
Makes about 4 dozen cookies

These little, barely sweet cookies from Frantoio Restaurant in Mill Valley, California, are delicious with sorbet, sliced fruit, or with an espresso at the end of a meal. They are crisp and have a delightful graininess. I even love them for breakfast with a cappuccino.

$2\frac{1}{4}$ cups all-purpose flour

1 tablespoon baking powder

$1\frac{1}{2}$ cups fine-grained polenta

1 tablespoon ground cinnamon

$\frac{3}{4}$ cup sugar

2 medium eggs

3 tablespoons honey

$\frac{1}{3}$ cup whole, low-fat, or nonfat milk

Finely minced zest of 2 lemons (about 3 tablespoons)

$\frac{1}{2}$ cup mild extra-virgin olive oil

Sugar for sprinkling

Preheat an oven to 350 degrees F. Oil 2 baking sheets with olive oil.

In a large mixing bowl, combine the flour, baking powder, polenta, cinnamon, and $\frac{3}{4}$ cup sugar and stir with a wooden spoon to integrate the ingredients. Then add the eggs, honey, milk, lemon zest, and olive oil. Stir to combine well. The dough will be slightly sticky. Scoop up teaspoonfuls of the dough and form "coins," flattening the dough with the back of a spoon or the palm of your hand. Arrange on the prepared baking sheets, spacing them about 1 inch apart. They will spread slightly during baking.

Bake until golden, about 20 minutes. Remove from the oven and sprinkle with sugar. Using a spatula, transfer to a wire rack to cool, tapping off any excess sugar. These cookies can be stored in an airtight container for up to 1 week.

Orange Ginger Cake

Makes one 8-inch cake; serves 8 to 10

An 8-inch springform cake pan works best for this cake, but an 8-inch cake pan lined with parchment paper or oiled waxed paper will do. I had a version of this cake in Provence a long time ago, and had tried to duplicate it for years. Then I came across food writer Michele Scicolone's recipe and adapted it by adding the candied ginger.

²⁄₃ cup fresh orange juice

¹⁄₂ cup honey

¹⁄₄ mild extra-virgin olive oil

2 eggs, at room temperature, separated

4 teaspoons shredded orange zest

5 tablespoons very thinly sliced candied ginger

1²⁄₃ cups all-purpose flour

¹⁄₂ cup granulated sugar

1 teaspoon baking powder

¹⁄₂ teaspoon salt

2 tablespoons confectioners' sugar

Preheat an oven to 350 degrees F. Oil an 8-inch springform pan with olive oil, dust with flour, and tap out excess flour.

In a medium-sized bowl, stir together the orange juice, honey, olive oil, egg yolks, 3 teaspoons of the orange zest, and 3 tablespoons of the candied ginger. In a large bowl, sift together the flour, granulated sugar, baking powder, and salt. In yet another medium-sized bowl, beat the egg whites until soft peaks form.

Using a wooden spoon, stir the orange juice mixture into the flour mixture. Using a spatula, gently fold in the egg whites until they are well integrated. Pour the batter into the prepared pan.

Bake until a toothpick inserted into the center of the cake comes out clean, 45 minutes to 1 hour. Transfer the pan to a wire rack to cool for 10 minutes. Remove the sides of the pan and let the cake cool completely. Sift the confectioners' sugar evenly over the top, then sprinkle on the remaining 1 teaspoon zest. Decorate with the remaining 2 tablespoons candied ginger.

If you wrap the cake in plastic wrap, it tastes even better the second day. Decorate with the confectioners' sugar, zest, and ginger just before serving.

Fried Cheese with Honey, Walnuts, and Cinnamon

Serves 4

Christophoros Veneris serves this dessert at Veneto, his restaurant in Heraklion, Crete. It is the perfect mix of savory and sweet, especially after one of his delicious meals of lots of fish, cooked greens, and stuffed eggplant. As an appetizer, Greek fried cheese is called *saganaki*, named for the two-handled shallow pan in which it is traditionally cooked and served.

12 to 16 walnut halves

½ pound ketalotiri or a hard pecorino-type cheese

⅓ cup ouzo or dry white wine

4 to 5 tablespoons all-purpose flour

About ¼ cup extra-virgin olive oil, preferably Greek

6 tablespoons sage honey or any good imported honey

Ground cinnamon for sprinkling

Preheat an oven to 350 degrees F. Spread the walnut halves on a baking sheet and toast in the oven until fragrant, 8 to 10 minutes. Remove from the oven and let cool.

Cut the cheese into 4-inch squares. Pour the ouzo or white wine into a shallow bowl. Put the flour into another shallow bowl. Dip each square of cheese into the liquid, then dust with the flour, shaking off the excess.

In a small, heavy skillet (or a *saganaki* pan, if you have one), pour in enough of the olive oil to generously cover the bottom of the pan. Warm it over medium heat until it is hot. Add the cheese, a few pieces at a time. Let the cheese brown, then turn it over and brown on the second side, 1 to 2 minutes on each side. Repeat with the remaining cheese, adding more olive oil as needed. The amount of oil you will use will depend upon the size of the pan. Using a slotted spoon, transfer to a wire rack placed over paper towels to drain.

Arrange the hot cheese on a serving platter and drizzle with the honey. Scatter the walnuts on top and sprinkle lightly with the cinnamon. Serve warm or at room temperature.

Sweet Fried Crisps
Makes 20 or 40 crisps

Sometimes called Alicante rags in Spain, these quick, light crisps are a delightful dessert to accompany fresh fruit or ice cream. They take minutes to make. Fry them early in the day and leave them unwrapped until it's time to eat them, or fry them just before serving. If you keep the temperature of the oil at a constant 365 degrees F, and drain the crisps on a rack instead of on paper towels, they will be absolutely nongreasy and perfectly crisp. Look for the wonton wrappers in Chinese groceries or well-stocked supermarkets.

About 1 cup bulk mild
    extra-virgin olive oil

20 thin square wonton
    wrappers

Cinnamon sugar, confection-
    ers' sugar, or honey

Pour the olive oil into a heavy skillet or a deep-fat fryer to a depth of about 2^1/$_2$ inches and heat to 365 degrees F. Leave the wonton wrappers whole, or cut them in half on the diagonal. When the oil is ready, using tongs and working in batches, carefully lower the wrappers into the hot oil. When they start to turn golden, after a minute or two, remove them from the oil with tongs and drain on a wire rack placed over paper towels.

Transfer the crisps to a platter, mounding them. Sprinkle with cinnamon sugar or confectioners' sugar or drizzle with honey. They can be served hot or they can be cooked a few hours ahead of time, left unwrapped, and served at room temperature.

Sources

CORTI BROTHERS
5810 Folsom Boulevard
Sacramento, CA 95819
800-509-3663
Wide variety of olive oils, vinegars, truffles, salted anchovies and capers.

DEAN & DELUCA
MAIL-ORDER DEPARTMENT
560 Broadway
New York, NY 10012
800-221-7714, ext. 270
212-226-6800
Wide selection of olive oils; squid ink.

FRANTOIO
152 Shoreline Highway
Mill Valley, CA 94941
415-289-5770
California cold-pressed, unfiltered olive oils pressed on premises; Imported Tuscan oil, Ugnana, from proprietor's estate

GRAY'S GRIST MILL
P.O. Box 422
Adamsville, RI 02801
509-636-6075
Polenta and stone-ground flours.

KALUSTYAN
123 Lexington Avenue
New York, NY 10016
212-685-3416
Harissa and Middle Eastern foods.

KATZ & CO.
101 South Coombs-Y3
Napa, CA 94559
800-455-2305
707-254-1866
fax 707-254-1846
Specializes in California olive oils, usually about twenty varieties; some European estate-bottled oils.

LA ESPANOLA
25020 Doble Avenue
Harbor City, CA 90710
310-539-0455
Spanish products including Spanish sausages, squid ink, paella pans, earthenware pots.

THE OIL MERCHANT
47 Ashchurch Grove
London, W12 9BU, England
0181 740 1335
fax 0181 740 1319
Excellent mail-order source in Britain; good variety, intelligently selected.

THE PASTA SHOP
5655 College Avenue
Oakland, CA 94618
510-547-4005
fax 510-601-8251
Inventory of at least fifty extra-virgin olive oils and other supplies.

STRICTLY OLIVE OIL
916 Ruth Court
Pacific Grove, CA 93950
408-372-6682
Conducts olive oil seminars and tastings; will advise about olive oil and will ship.

NICK SCIABICA & SONS
2150 Yosemite Boulevard
Modesto, CA 953541
800-551-9612
209-577-5067
fax 209-524-5367
Inventory of fourteen varietal California extra-virgin olive oils, and an additional three unfiltered California extra-virgin oils.

SUR LA TABLE
410 Terry Avenue North
Seattle, WA 98109-5229
206-682-7175
Olio Extra Vergine Buonsapore (Stephen Singer's import, the oil used at Chez Panisse) and other oils.

VINEGAR FACTORY
431 East 91th Street
New York, NY 10128
212-987-0885
Usually carries Portuguese oil; has a regularly changing selection of excellent oils (no mail-order services).

VIVANDE PORTA VIA
2125 Fillmore Street
San Francisco, CA 94115
415-346-4430
415-346-2877
Carries more than fifteen imported Italian oils, a few Spanish and specialty oils, salted capers.

WALLY'S
2107 Westwood Bouvelard
Los Angeles, CA 90025
310-475-0606
800-892-5597
fax 310-474-1450
An inventory of about fifty oils.

WILLIAMS SONOMA
Mail-order Department
P.O. Box 7456
San Francisco, CA 94120-7456
800-541-2233
Changing variety of olive oils, mainly available after harvest.

ZINGERMAN'S DELICATESSEN
422 Detroit Street
Ann Arbor, MI 48104-3400
313-769-1625
fax 313-769-1235
Large selection of olive oils, Calispara rice, salted capers.

Bibliography

Algar, Ayla. *Classical Turkish Cooking*. New York: Harper Collins, 1991.

Bertolli, Paul, and Alice Waters. *Chez Panisse Cooking*. New York: Random House, 1988.

Casas, Penelope. *Discovering Spain, an Uncommon Guide*. New York: Alfred A. Knopf, 1996.

Cunningham, Marion. *The Fannie Farmer Cookbook*. New York: Alfred A. Knopf, 1990.

Dolamore, Anne. *A Buyer's Guide to Olive Oil*. London: Grub Street, 1994.

———. *The Essential Olive Oil Companion*. New York: Interlink Books, 1988.

Field, Carol. *The Italian Baker*. New York: Harper & Row, 1985.

Goldstein, Joyce. *The Mediterranean Kitchen*. New York: William Morrow, 1989.

Gray, Patience. *Honey from a Weed*. New York: Harper & Row, 1986.

Hazan, Marcella. *Essentials of Classic Italian Cooking*. New York: Alfred A. Knopf, 1992.

Jenkins, Nancy Harmon. *The Mediterranean Diet Cookbook*. New York: Bantam Books, 1994.

Jordan, Michele Anna. *The Good Cook's Book of Oil & Vinegar*. Reading, MA: Addison-Wesley Publishing, 1992.

Klein, Maggie. *The Feast of the Olive*. San Francisco: Chronicle Books, 1994.

Kochilas, Diane. *The Food and Wine of Greece*. New York: St. Martin's Press, 1990.

Kremezi, Aglaia. *The Foods of Greece*. New York: Stewart, Tabori & Chang, 1993.

Midgley, John. *The Goodness of Olive Oil*. New York: Random House, 1992.

Olive Oil, a Guide for Culinary Professionals. Madrid: International Council of Olive Oil; and Hyde Park, NY: The Culinary Institute of America, 1996.

Olney, Richard. *LuLu's Provençal Table*. New York: Harper Collins, 1994.

Rogers, Ford. *Olives, Cooking with Olives and Their Oils*. Berkeley: Ten Speed Press, 1995.

Root, Waverly. *The Food of France*. New York: Alfred A. Knopf, 1958.

———. *The Food of Italy*. New York: Atheneum, 1971.

Seed, Diane. *Italian Cooking with Olive Oil*. New York: William Morrow, 1995.

Weinzweig, Ari. *A Guide to Good Olive Oil*. Ann Arbor, MI: Zingerman's, 1995.

Wolfert, Paula. *The Cooking of the Eastern Mediterranean*. New York: Harper Collins, 1994.

———. *Couscous and Other Good Food From Morocco*. New York: Harper & Row, 1974.

———. *Mediterranean Cooking*. New York: Ecco Press, 1982.

———. *Paula Wolfert's World of Food*. New York: Harper & Row, 1988.

Index

OLIVE OIL · FROM TREE TO TABLE

INDEX

OLIVE OIL · FROM TREE TO TABLE

Table of Equivalents

—❧—

The exact equivalents in the following tables have been rounded for convenience.

ABBREVIATIONS

US

oz=ounce
lb=pound
in=inch
ft=foot
tbl=tablespoon
fl oz=fluid ounce
qt=quart

METRIC

g=gram
kg=kilogram
mm=millimeter
cm=centimeter
ml=milliliter
l=liter

WEIGHTS

US/UK	METRIC
1 oz	30 g
2 oz	60 g
3 oz	90 g
4 oz ($^1/_4$ lb)	125 g
5 oz ($^1/_3$ lb)	155 g
6 oz	185 g
7 oz	220 g
8 oz ($^1/_2$ lb)	250 g
10 oz	315 g
12 oz ($^3/_4$ lb)	375 g
14 oz	440 g
16 oz (1 lb)	500 g
$1^1/_2$ lbs	750 g
2 lbs	1 kg
3 lbs	1.5 kg

OVEN TEMPERATURES

FAHRENHEIT	CELSIUS	GAS
250	120	$^1/_2$
275	140	1
300	150	2
325	160	3
350	180	4
375	190	5
400	200	6
425	220	7
450	230	8
475	240	9
500	260	10

LIQUIDS

US	METRIC	UK
2 tbl	30 ml	1 fl oz
$^1/_4$ cup	60 ml	2 fl oz
$^1/_3$ cup	80 ml	3 fl oz
$^1/_2$ cup	125 ml	4 fl oz
$^2/_3$ cup	160 ml	5 fl oz
$^3/_4$ cup	180 ml	6 fl oz
1 cup	250 ml	8 fl oz
$1^1/_2$ cups	375 ml	12 fl oz
2 cups	500 ml	16 fl oz

167